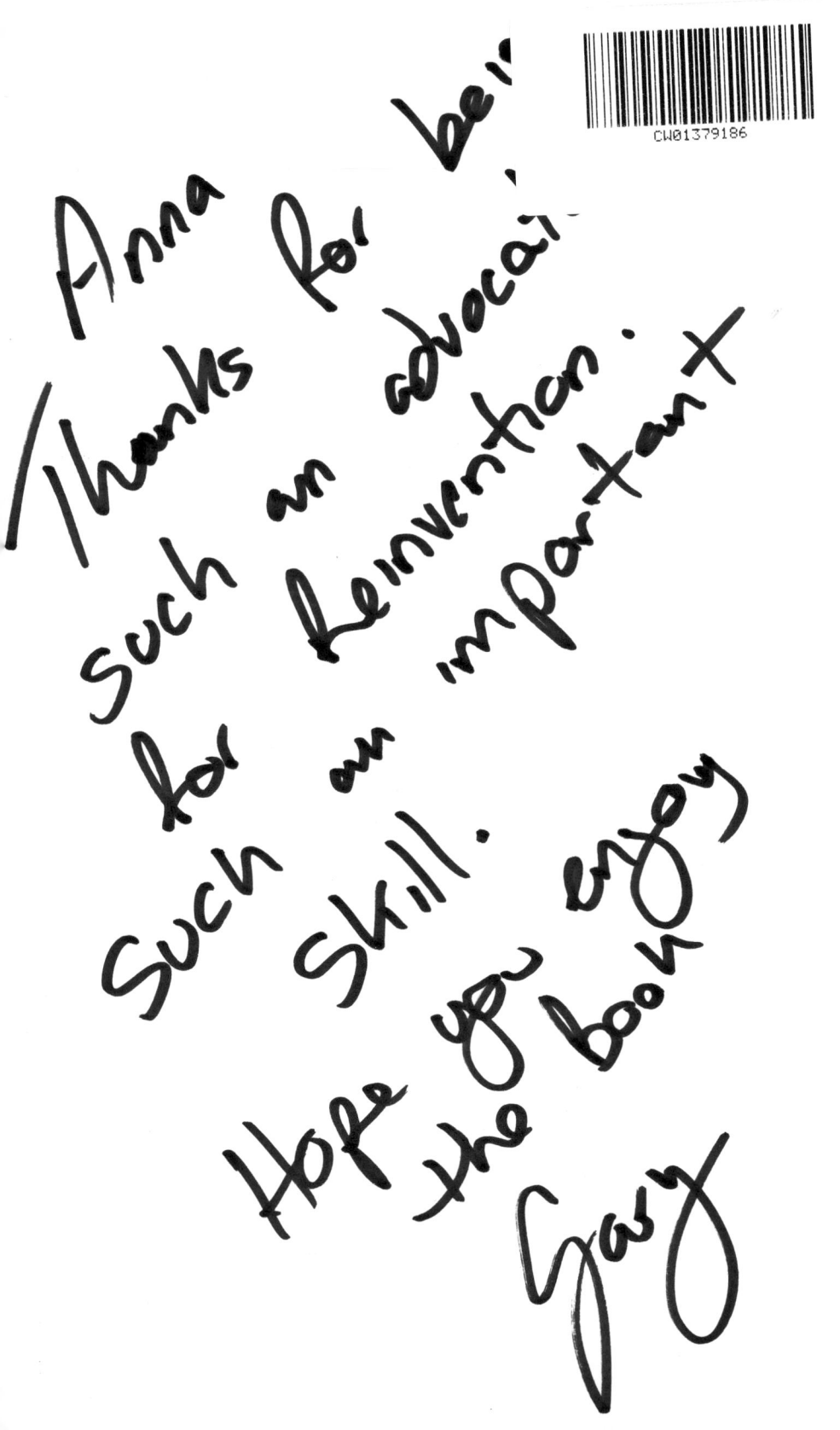

Anna
Thanks for be[ing]
such an advoca[te]
for Reinvention.
such an important
skill.
Hope you enjoy
the book
Gary

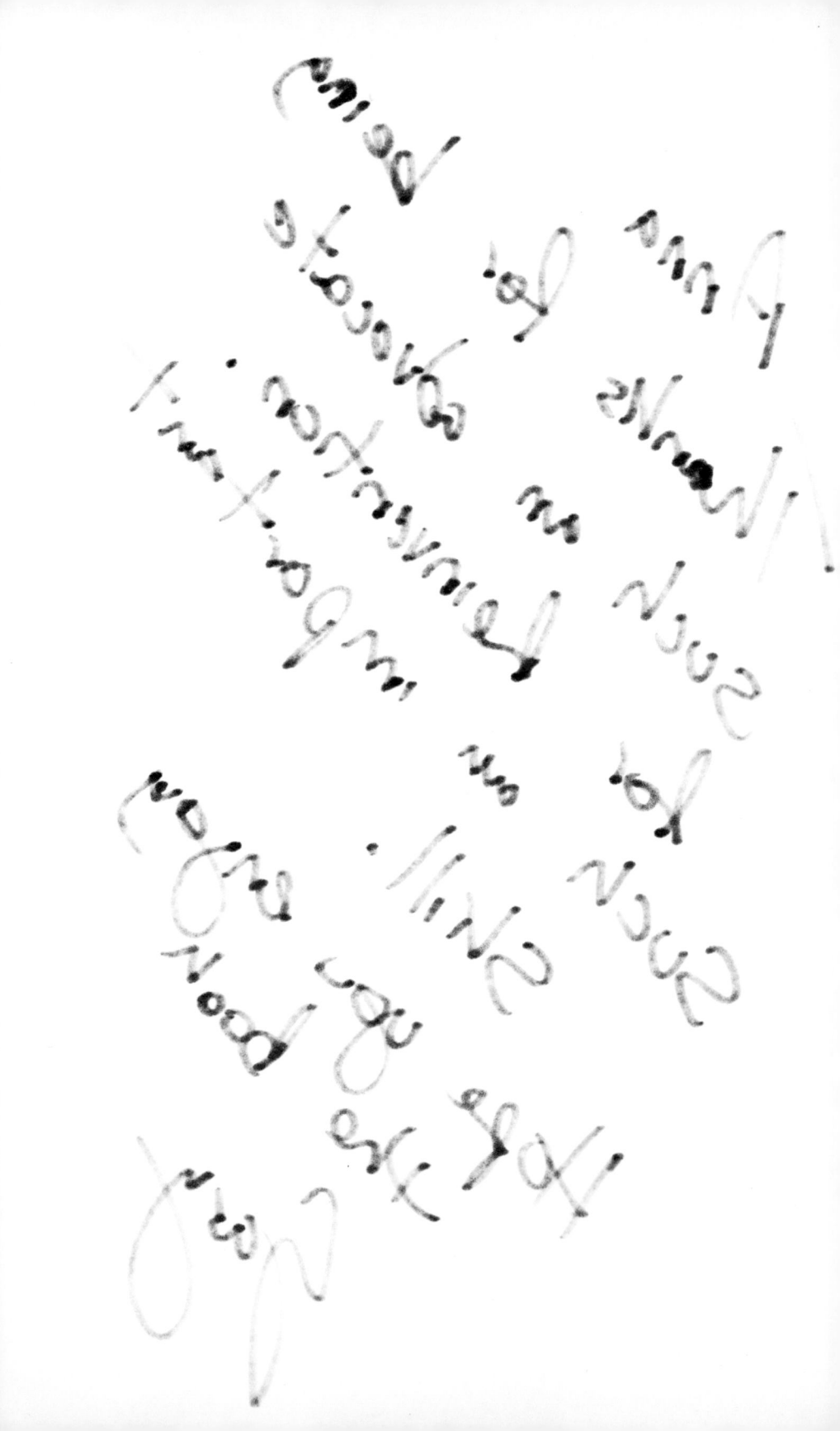

Thanks for being
such an advocate
for an handwriter.
Such an important
skill. Hope you
have a good day
Meg

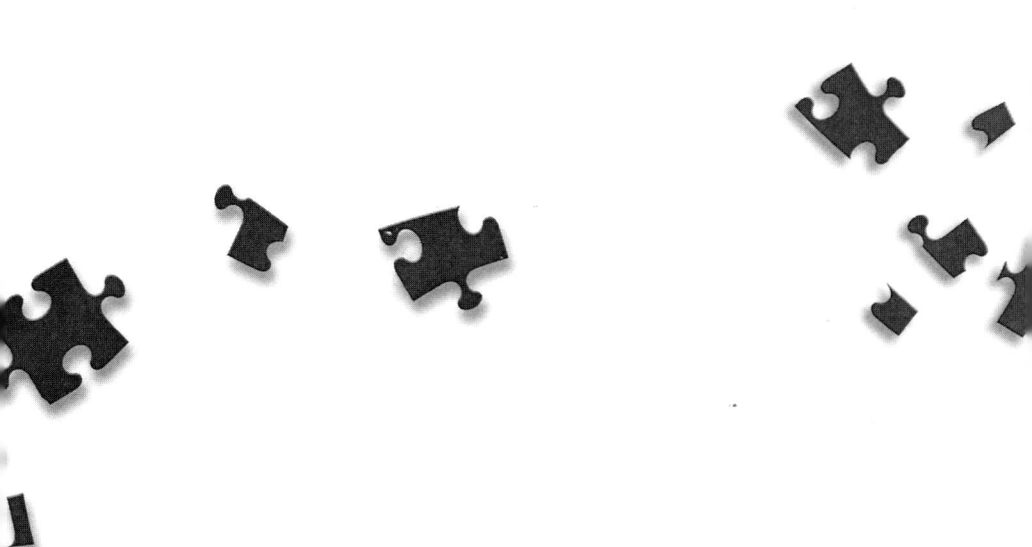

MASTERING THE ART OF
REINVENTION

MASTERING THE ART OF
REINVENTION

Copyright © 2025 Gary Waldon.
Do Good Sh!t Publishing Pty Ltd

First published in Australia 2025
Copyright © Gary Waldon 2025

The right of Gary Waldon to be identified as the Author of the Work has been asserted in accordance with the Copyright, Designs and Patents Act 1988.

All rights reserved. No part of this publication may be reproduced, stored in a retrieval system, or transmitted, in any form or by any means without the prior written permission of the publisher, nor be otherwise circulated in any form of binding or cover other than that in which it is published and without a similar condition being imposed on the subsequent purchaser.

For information:

Do Good Sh!t Publishing Pty Ltd,
hello@garywaldon.com

Printed by Paradigm Print Media

Editor: Penny Carroll
Design: Michael McDermaid
Proof reading: Teagan Kum Sing
Publicity: Scott Eathorne, quikmarkmedia.com.au

ISBN: 978-0-6488320-2-7 (paperback)
ISBN: 978-0-6488320-3-4 (eBook)

MASTERING THE ART OF REINVENTION

ADAPTING TO LIFE, AI AND OTHER BIG CHANGES

GARY WALDON

Contents

Foreword - Dr Dinesh Palipana OAM 8
Foreword - Craig Stowers 10
Introduction 12
The art of reinvention 20

Stage 1: Change 27
F#ck change 29
Holy crap! 34
Change influencers 44
AI - A generational change 53
Why me? The emotions of change 61

Stage 2: Reality Check 69
Losing control 71
This too shall pass 77
The good, the bad and the ugly 82

Stage 3: Empower Yourself 93
Let's bounce 95
Writing your life story 100
Which way? 107
Facing fears (fears blame and loathing) 114

Stage 4: Action 123
- Do something, anything 125
- Think big, start small 132
- Road trip! 137
- Coffee, Coke and other habits 142

Stage 5: Try, then Try Again 151
- Keep chipping away 153
- Cover your bases 160
- Beware of comparisonitis 167

Stage 6: Enjoy the Journey 173
- Be kind to yourself and others 175
- Let yourself go 181
- Do good sh!t 187
- Conclusion 190

Masters of Reinvention 195
- Angie Simpson 197
- Tony Nash 201
- Dr Dinesh Palipana OAM 206

- Acknowledgements 213
- About the Author 216
- The Gig Game 218

Foreword

DR DINESH PALIPANA OAM,
AUTHOR OF *STRONGER*

It has been a privilege to get to come to know Gary over a period of time. In this world, we need people who are passionate, kind, and see things as they can be – not a cog in the machine of how things are. To me, this is Gary.

In Sri Lanka, which has a large Buddhist population, Buddhism is frequently taught to children. As I was growing up there for the first ten years of life, this philosophy was taught to me too. One of the teachings of Buddhism is that everything is the impermanence of things.

Change. It's the only constant.

I have come to learn this all too well throughout the time on this earth.

In 1994, we moved from a war-torn country at the age of ten. We moved through different cities. I've been to nearly ten different schools in my life. I studied law, then was inspired to study medicine after depression. In medical school, I had a spinal cord injury which changed life forever. I was paralysed from the chest down.

Change. It's the only constant.

The world around us changes all the time. But, we change too. We realise this if we reflect on the old saying, "no steps in the same river twice".

Buddhism also teaches that attachment is one of the leading causes of suffering. For me, some ingredients to happiness have been to embrace change, to expect change, and not to be attached to things.

This is what Gary's book *Mastering the Art of Reinvention* is about. He weaves a rich tapestry through some philosophies of life, about understanding change, and the role technology plays in that journey.

I have learned that we are social creatures who are stronger together. Together, we thrive. Together, we innovate. Together, we create a better world. That is why, as I have been given the honour of making a small contribution to Gary's word, that I am thrilled to introduce you to *Mastering the Art of Reinvention*.

Foreword

CRAIG STOWERS

"Who is this guy?" was my thought as I walked away from the gym after my initial meeting with Gary and the promise of a book he had written. Little did I realise that this distinguished-looking gentleman would be a part of the catalyst that I needed to really help me. When we met, I was a walking cliché, a bad walking cliché. I was a middle aged, balding, obese, depressed, recent divorcee who honestly was second guessing the decision to NOT try out the toaster as a bath toy (and a new hand tattoo to enforce that decision thankfully).

Sort Your Sh!t Out in bold print was what I read as he handed me that book. The title grabbed me straight away, those four words encapsulated the journey I was on perfectly. I could say that the book changed my world view and reading it made my life instantly better and farted nothing but rainbows since, but that would be a lie. The truth is the book was confronting. Gary's ability to express his thoughts and experiences in a humorous manner struck the right chord and it felt like the universe had conspired to help me, or maybe it was Seb, Gary's Personal Trainer and my BJJ coach. On top of the book was Gary's friendship. From initial acknowledgment and awkward nods to greetings of the manliest of man-hugs, his insight or carefully crafted questions would lead me down another path on my journey.

When Gary asked me to write this foreword, I was honoured but also perplexed on why the hell he would want me to do it. He has access and friendships with Olympic champions, celebrated and highly achieved individuals from around the world and other remarkable masters of reinvention. I've had the manuscript for two days and am writing this in the wee hours of Sunday morning. As I was pondering and reflecting on what I have just read, I realised in the past 12 months through the guidance and wisdom (minus his love of bell bottoms and man buns) he graciously, fortunately and thankfully imparted on me the very lessons that he has distilled in this book *Mastering the Art of Reinvention*.

I am looking in a mirror, and the face I see staring back at me isn't the same as what was there. I no longer see the same cliché. I see someone who has become positive, adaptable, determined and accepting if not welcoming of change. So, while looking in the mirror and contemplating Gary and his influence on mine and many other lives I am left pondering.

"Who is this guy?"

Introduction

"Life's a puzzle, and sometimes you just have to put the pieces together in a new way".

— The Riddler (*Batman: Arkham Knight*)

When we start a new puzzle, we tip all the pieces out and then try to figure out where each piece fits. We all have our own approach to puzzles: some of us start at the corners, as they are easy to identify, others turn the picture on the box upside down so we have to figure out where the pieces fit by trying them. When we start there can be thousands of pieces scattered before us, then over time we find pieces that are a perfect fit, other pieces that seem to almost fit and then there are the pieces that just don't belong. The closer we get to finishing it the more we get attached to it, because of the time we committed to creating this masterpiece.

The tricky thing about life is that we get attached to the picture we have spent so much time building. We've spent years fitting the pieces together – work, relationships and our identity – assuming our puzzle will eventually make sense. But what if the picture itself keeps changing? What if the edges shift, new pieces appear, and some of the ones you were so sure about no longer fit at all? Reinvention isn't just about choice; sometimes, it's about survival. The world doesn't sit still just because we're not ready for it to change. We've seen it before – industries evolving, entire ways of life disappearing overnight. And yet, it always seems to catch us off guard. We assume the rules we live by will always stay the same, right up until the moment they don't.

Think back to 2020 when COVID hit and the way the rules, as we understood them, changed beyond recognition. I remember wandering around my local supermarket looking for the latest specials and checking the price of toilet paper for the best buys, that was if I could find any due to the irrational panic buying people were doing.

There were all these new faces of people stacking shelves and manning the checkouts. As I watched them diligently going about their jobs, I wondered about the paths that had led them to their current careers.

In Australia, we took an aggressive approach to managing the COVID threat. The entire country was locked down for a while, decimating many industries and, as a result, people's businesses, careers, incomes and lives were shattered. Aviation, hospitality and public-facing businesses were stopped from trading and employees were being let go en masse.

A good friend's daughter had been a pilot for Virgin Australia. At 20, she was a second officer flying the Australia–Los Angeles return route. She was enjoying all the trappings that came with a starting salary of $100,000-plus per year, which could grow to way over $300,000 as her career progressed. She had bought a new car and, sensibly, she was looking to buy her first property.

Before COVID, things were more than rosy for her. She was living the dream.

I thought about her as I paid for my groceries and wondered how many of these new employees were from airlines or other impacted industries. I reflected on how I was always so impressed with the uniforms flight crew wore with such pride. People looked up to them with respect and admiration and they were able to create lives that matched their high incomes – nice cars, luxury houses, multiple investment properties and surplus income to support holidays and purchasing life's niceties. With their glamorous jobs no longer in existence, many reluctantly had to look for ways to survive. Supermarkets were busier than ever (toilet paper sales included) and were one of the few industries hiring at that time. Among the new recruits there were no doubt some fortunate pilots who had been able to accept their new reality, swallowing their pride and taking any job that kept them afloat until things changed, as they always eventually do.

Now jump forward to 2024, with AI (Artificial Intelligence) hurtling towards us like an out-of-control asteroid. As I always do, I shared this book with a good friend of mine, Craig, to review and he asked me why I included AI in a self-help book. He said he doesn't even use ChatGPT or any of the other AI tools, so it seemed out of context. For Craig his world hasn't started to feel the impacts of AI, and as a result hasn't contemplated his future world with AI playing a large part. His reaction probably isn't unique, many of us will be caught off guard by AI as it is still in the early stages and may feel like it is something alien that is happening outside of our personal world.

However, collision with humanity is unavoidable now, and the impacts on our way of life are evolving and largely unknown. The dooms-dayers amongst us believe this new AI world threatens to displace humanity's role and identity in our world. There are fears that over the next five years millions of jobs will be lost as AI becomes smarter than even the most brilliant humans or that even robots can do most of the things more efficiently and safer than humans. The AI optimists in this evolving commentary portray a future where we have more leisure time, human diseases and conditions have all been cured and we can chase our dreams without the burden of having to work or worry about the more mundane aspects of life. Regardless of whether the impact of AI is positive or negative, our lives are going through a generational transformation and as a result our identities will also change forever.

I reflected on how these two life-changing events, AI and COVID, forced many of us to deal with the resulting identity crisis. As we know now, the mental health issues that resulted from the enforced, unwelcome COVID changes will be with us for decades. The impact was dependent on how agile, willing and able people were to adapt to their new reality.

While the plight of humanity is what resonated with me, it is worth remembering that every person around the globe is going through their own challenges and adjusting to their 'new normal' every single day. Although most media focuses on the impacts of big societal changes such as AI, COVID or other big events, the need or desire for people to reinvent themselves can be attributed to any one of a million other things, both big and small.

As a science teacher, I would set up fun experiments in which a certain mix of chemicals would make foam spurt out of test tubes. I remember the *oohs* and *aahs* of my suitably impressed students. I felt like a master magician.

Just as with chemistry, in our everyday world, we experience more personal catalysts that impact our lives to varying degrees every minute. Some are minor, such as choosing what to wear on a cold rainy day; others are life-changing events, such as finding out a partner has been cheating, losing a job, being injured in a car accident, going bankrupt or simply becoming frustrated with life and deciding to make a change.

Some catalysts, such as losing a job, may demand we change immediately, while others can build and build until we can't take it anymore, like a relationship that has outlived the attraction it was originally built on.

I chose *Mastering the Art of Reinvention* as the title of this book because while life, and how we interact with it, continually requires us to change and evolve, there is an art to how we reinvent ourselves to not only survive, but more importantly thrive in the new world we find ourselves. An artist is someone who creates their masterpieces using their unique perspectives, based on combining their past experiences and outlooks, as well as their skill, whether it be painting, drawing, sculpting or, in our case, reinventing our lives.

The *Cambridge Dictionary* defines *invention* as "something that has never been made before, or the process of creating something that has never been made before" and reinvention as "that act of producing something new that is based on something that already exists".

As much as we sometimes wish that we could reboot our lives and start with a clean slate, with our past mistakes wiped out and forgotten, we can't, not yet anyway. Any change we make in our lives leverages where we have come from and who we are.

When I released my last book, *Sort Your Sh!t Out*, in August 2020, we were still coming to terms with how COVID had changed our world. *Sort Your Sh!t Out* focused on how our minds create much of the shit impacting us and holding us back. My PR guy reassured me that the timing was perfect to help people *sort their shit out* and we attracted great interest from the media. Being no one famous, I was delighted to be presented with these opportunities to promote my book and talk about how it could help people cope with the resulting mental health issues.

But much to my bemusement, readers were more interested in the 43 different jobs I had held throughout my life. After starting out as a milkman, I had been paid to do jobs as diverse as teaching, lecturing at university, topless waiting, modelling and consulting to CEOs. There were online news stories, national television appearances and radio interviews all about how I had redefined and reinvented myself so many times.

Some joked that I wasn't able to stick to anything (possibly true); others wanted to chat about my time as a topless waiter and why I never made it to the great heights of male stripping (my dad dance moves aren't sexy, or so I'm told); but, ultimately, the essence of their focus was on how I reinvented myself so many times. Given the rapidly-changing world we are living in, this formed the catalyst for me to write this book.

I have made a very successful career from reinvention, transformation and change. I have been responsible for creating banks for famous people, commissioned hospitals, delivered COVID-19 contact-tracing systems for health professionals and created several startups. I have failed and succeeded, been hired and fired (rarely both in the same day), and along the way I became a master of reinvention. In all these endeavours, I came to realise that from the day we are born to the day we die, we are continually reinventing ourselves. You are not the person you were yesterday, and the things that happen today will make you a different person tomorrow.

Right down to a cellular level, we are continually reinventing ourselves. The average age of the cells in the human body is seven to ten years. This means that nearly every cell in your body is replaced with new cells during this period. Skin cells last only 14 days, while some neuronal cells in the brain and the cells that make up your eyes aren't renewed at all. The same is true for how we react to change. Some aspects of us are more open and adaptable to change, like our willingness to embrace the latest fashion trends, while other aspects, like our core values and beliefs, require far greater effort to shift.

While we are made for reinvention, any renewal comes with uncertainty. We may believe we are masters of today, or hope to become masters in the future, but there are no guarantees that we will excel tomorrow. This is where our reluctance to change kicks in. Our inherent fear of failure makes us focus on what could go wrong rather than what could go right.

Sir David Attenborough, in his documentary *A Life on Our Planet*, talks about the five catastrophic events in the history of the Earth that have led to mass extinctions. He notes: "I learned that every 100 million years or so, something catastrophic happened – a mass extinction, caused by a profound, rapid, global change to the environment to which so many species had become adapted." In our lifetimes we will experience profound and rapid life changes that will require us to adapt, refocus and reinvent ourselves, and fortunately we will experience frequent periods of stability in which we create new habits that may be tested again by the next life change.

This is exactly what is happening to us right now with AI at a societal level. To avoid becoming irrelevant and outdated or even worse, becoming extinct, we need to adapt by mastering the art of reinvention. Throughout the book I have approached AI as just another life changing event that demands our reinvention. *Mastering the Art of Reinvention* is about helping build the necessary skills to adapt to all changes. If you are wanting to learn about AI, which I strongly recommend you do, I suggest jumping online and exploring it. With the incredible pace of change being experienced with AI it is impossible for any book to be able to provide you a current view of the AI state of play.

The art of reinvention

As a kid, I had a big box full of colourful Lego pieces of all shapes and sizes. From out of this mess, I would build all sorts of masterpieces. Sitting on the floor, I would assemble blocks into skyscrapers, animals, robots, planes, cars, dinosaurs and a seemingly endless array of weird-looking, but in my eyes, perfect, creations. The only limitation was my imagination. And when I wanted to create my next invention, I would pull the pieces apart and start again.

The possibilities were endless. I was always fascinated that when my friends and I agreed (albeit reluctantly at times) to build the same objects, the end creations always differed so much. Lego is like real life when it comes to reinvention. What you create is only limited by your imagination, drive and resilience. Just because you built one version of yourself, doesn't mean you can't change it later down the line.

All the pieces of you are already in the box. But who's to say we can't change and reinvent ourselves? COVID-19 was one of the biggest catalysts for change I have seen in my life, and we are moving into the next one now with AI. During the early stages of the pandemic, I managed a team of great people who were responsible for designing software to support contact tracing across Queensland, Australia. I felt humbled to be able to contribute to keeping people safe and I was also fascinated about how this virus could be non-existent one day and running rampant throughout the human population the next. What was the catalyst, I wondered?

Epidemiologists introduced me to the concept of *shift* and *drift*. Like us, virus cells are in a constant state of change. Most of the time, life is a series of small changes, as we and the virus cells *drift* through life. We stay in our little worlds and changes are often so minimal we hardly notice them. Then something happens that causes a jump or *shift* in who we are. In the case of COVID-19, the virus reportedly evolved into a strain that could jump from animals (most likely bats, it seems) to humans. Our lives went from being normal to completely messed up and, as time passed, we found our new normal. AI is about to throw all of the cards back into the air again, so our reinvention skills will be called on once more.

This is the wonderful adaptability of humans. We are survivors. Depending on our mindset, we can adapt to all sorts of situations. Humans live in the harshest deserts right through to the sub-polar temperatures of the Artic. Yet not all humans always adapt. While some people may survive, there are those who can't, or are unwilling, to change.

When faced with challenges, we are also presented with choices and opportunities. The movie *127 Hours*, starring James Franco, tells the incredible story of Aron Ralston, a mountaineer whose arm was trapped under a huge boulder when he slipped during a hike. When he couldn't free himself, he was faced with the choice of living or dying. He chose to live and cut off his lower arm. His survival instinct was so strong that enduring the pain of cutting through his arm with a blunt knife was better than giving up and dying.

While I'm not sure I could do what Aron Ralston did, I do know I have a strong survival instinct, and so do most of us. Physiologically, we are designed to survive, but sometimes our heads overrule our survival instinct and convince us to give up. This is where resilience comes in – this is the quality that enables us to pick ourselves up again and again when we get knocked down. Cue the chorus of the 1997 hit "Tubthumping" by Chumbawamba.

I must apologise as this song is likely to get stuck in your head for days now.

Mastering the Art of Reinvention is a guide to help you get back up when life has knocked you down. This book will help you create the new, (hopefully) improved version of yourself and teach you how to design and own your new normal so you can thrive in the future. I am not selling you the dream of "everything will be perfect, and life will turn out exactly how you want it to". Rather, this is a book about how to survive the ups and downs of life without getting lost in the darkness, so you can make the best of each opportunity when it arrives.

Former rugby great Tim Horan says: "Keep chipping away on the field so that when the break comes, you can go for it and score the goal." *Mastering the Art of Reinvention* is about getting you ready for that break and preparing you to go for the win once the break presents itself. Not every play will result in us scoring a try.

Reinvention is about how we CREATE the next version of ourselves, which comprises of our physical, mental, emotional and social aspects as well as our career and financial state.

The six stages of CREATE are:

Change: Change happens, whether we like it or not. However, not all change is the result of external forces. Sometimes we simply decide that our normal is not working for us and it's time for a change. Change acceptance and readiness is not something that just happens; there is a process we must go through. Consider a relationship break-up: you don't usually go from being deliriously happy and in love to "it's over" in one night, unless something huge has happened. Other causes may come from outside our control or field of vision but still end up diverting our well-thought-out plans.

Reality check: When change happens, it causes a level of discomfort and uncertainty. The world we knew and the habits we created are all under threat. To ensure we get through the tough times, we should take stock, reflect and do a reality check. Ideally, we will focus on the things we can control and not waste energy on the things we can't. We also need to make a balance sheet of our lives by assessing the good, the bad and the ugly that have led us to this point. This will help us consciously decide what we want to create through this evolutionary process and where to focus our attention to create the next break.

Empower yourself: If we don't empower ourselves to get through whatever is impacting us right now to enable us to thrive, we end up leaving our lives to fate. We may buy a lottery ticket, grab a pizza, keep living our current lives and wait for our numbers to come up. A more productive use of our energy and brilliance is to identify what we're passionate about and then start figuring out how to get there. You might miss your old life, but you can't go back and, even if you could, you have changed and moved on. It will never fit you like it once did.

Action: Dreams and fairytales are great: they give us relief from the real world. Our actions and thoughts are often the only things within our control, so taking a planned approach to achieving our goals is critical to keeping us on track and motivated to overcome the inevitable obstacles that will come our way. To create a new life, we often need to break the habits we have built up in the past. For example, moving to a new house means finding a new route to work and where to grab the best coffee along the way.

Try, then try again: OK, tough love time. You are likely to fail along the way and end up somewhere different from where you thought you would be. Just like an infant learning to walk, you're on a journey of reinvention, trying new things and learning from your mistakes. Toddlers fall down, take stock, maybe even cry, then get back up and try again. Fear of failure exposes itself in many obscure ways: procrastination, anxiety, depression and avoidance are all symptoms of a fear of failure, which can derail our best plans and efforts. Getting your head on straight is about building the necessary resilience to try (and try again) and be kind to yourself when you fail.

Enjoy: Enjoy the journey, not just the destination. Some dear friends of mine, Tony and Wayne, delight in planning their travels.

They start months in advance and explore all the experiences their destinations offer. They know that their holiday will be over way too quickly, so they savour the journey of getting there almost as much as the location itself. Celebrating the little things along the way helps keep you motivated and on track so that when you hit a road bump, your energy levels and enthusiasm allow you to keep moving forward.

As someone who has helped many others transform their lives and workplaces you would think I love change. Nope! I actively resist change when I am not in control of the process. Using my understanding of the strong urge to resist change and combining it with my 40+ years of helping thousands realise their potential, I look forward to guiding you through the steps to creating the next version of you

Stage 1: Change

"Nothing is so painful to the human mind as a great and sudden change".

— Mary Shelley, *Frankenstein*

F#ck change

In my job helping organisations and their people deal with change, I have heard and seen many variations of the comment "fuck change" or the more polite version, "I hate change". Some are off the cuff, while others are passionate statements about their commitment to stay the same.

I'm usually called in when an organisation wants to take a new direction, or the business is underperforming. Regardless of the reason, the end result is that people and their jobs will need to change. When I start a new gig, I interview as many of the impacted people as I can to understand the situation and their views. As it starts to dawn on them that their world will change and they need to evolve or move on, a common phrase I hear is "no one likes change".

Most of us prefer to be in control of our own destiny, including how and when we change. So, I totally get the negativity. Although my job is to help others change, I fall into the category of people who hate it. I resist with every ounce of my energy when I'm forced to do something against my will. My wife knows when I'm not on board with a change by the way I reluctantly participate, looking for excuses and reasons to keep things as they are. Although she's usually right and the change does benefit me in the long run, I'll still drag my feet, and in some cases, I find ways to sabotage the change.

However, if I'm locked up at home in isolation, or have to eat the same thing more than twice in a row, even my favourite dish, or wear the same shirt every time I go out, then I'm likely to have a very different response to change. As much as I believe I would still look great with a man bun and have the ankles to wear bell-bottom flares, times have moved on and my tastes and preferences have evolved with them. And I could just imagine the revolt if I suggested to my wife that she should wear the same outfit twice in a row to a social event with our friends. She would be mortified at the thought of not being able to change her look with the fashions.

We eagerly consume the latest tech gadgets and phones when they're released, binge watch new shows, spend big on the latest fashions and fear the idea of being irrelevant. When we get the opportunity to choose, we will nearly always choose the latest and greatest, because we love change and like to be on the cutting edge.

The one common denominator about whether we love or hate change is how much control and influence we have over it. The less control we have, the more likely we are to resist and resent changes, even if they are in our best interests. AI is the perfect example of this, for most of us we believe we have little control over what is coming at us.

Let's say you decide to change the colour of your lounge room because you think it's out of date. A quick trip to the hardware store will help you visualise how the room will look using the latest colour cards. You purchase the paint, brushes and drop sheets. Once you finish the masterpiece, you stand back and congratulate yourself on the success of your changes. Now, imagine you did this without consulting your partner, and they liked the way the room used to look. If your household is anything like mine, there would be some heated discussions around "Don't you think it would have been good to talk to me first?", before you head straight back to the paint shop to find the original colour.

I remember one business I worked with where a group of around 50 people had been labelled as underperformers and whingers. Most of the team didn't want to be working there and many had used up their sick leave and holiday leave while looking for any excuse not to be in what they considered a caustic environment. In this example I'm referring to a workplace, however, this description could be applied to many situations, including home life and relationships. When I sat down with each of them individually, they were very vocal about how unhappy they were and how they wanted to find another job. Most had been worn down to the point where they thought the place couldn't be saved. Some told me they were actively looking for another job while the rest were looking but didn't come clean about it.

Fast forward a month or two and we had worked with the staff to find a better way of operating and had a plan to get them back to being the high-performance team they all had said they wanted to be a part of. Eagerly I watched their manager as he outlined the plan to turn their workplace around over the next 12 weeks, making sure he highlighted the benefits for them all. Then once again I sat down with many of them individually and this time they expressed their unhappiness and concern with the changes they were being made to endure. Even though they were desperately unhappy with the way things were, their fear of the unknown and their discomfort in being made to change and step out of the world they knew (and despised) created even higher levels of anxiety and stress, resulting in even more dysfunctional behaviours, with more threats to resign.

As humans, we're often rational in our behaviours and thoughts, but in the face of stressful situations we can become extremely irrational. When faced with the opportunity to improve an unhappy and stressful situation – such as a dysfunctional workplace, relationship or home life – we often choose to continue to suffer and endure, rather than risk stepping into the unknown.

Some of these workers were willing to quit and take lower-paying roles or become unemployed rather than live through the changes. The fear of the unknown was so overwhelming they were willing to put themselves through greater self-imposed pain to avoid it. This logic, or lack of it, is also why people stay in desperately unhappy relationships rather than make a change that could improve their quality of life. The irrational part is that their mind may be trying to convince them that they're better off wallowing in downright unpleasantness than enduring the discomfort of reinventing themselves.

So, it might be true that no one likes change, but I think a more accurate statement would be: "No one likes change, especially if they aren't in control."

Holy crap!

You're fired!

I'm leaving you!

You've failed!

You will never walk again!

You're bankrupt!

Aunt Jessie died and left you $10 million!

Any one of these statements are likely to trigger at least a "Holy crap!" response, as you realise your life will never be the same again. Your old normal is no more.

I'm not one to support the overuse of exclamation marks, but each of the above statements is "!" worthy. They are all life-changing events that demand our reinvention. Hopefully, this new version takes all the good things about us and builds on them, while leaving behind the stuff that wasn't serving us well, so we move forward into our future a better person.

With these opportunities for reinvention, we can choose between several paths. We can either do nothing, pretending nothing has happened, reluctantly approach the change or grab it with both hands and make the best of what we've been presented with. Regardless of how we respond, or whether we wanted the change or not, our action or inaction still represents a choice. Ignoring reality and hoping it goes away is making a choice.

Only the passing of time will reveal if the change is a catalyst for a better life or the start of a decline into tough times. Even winning the lottery doesn't guarantee a life of happiness and contentment as research shows that many winners regret their windfalls. The thrill of winning often turns into a nightmare, with friend's attitudes towards them changing and relationships breaking down. They often end up poorer than they were, both emotionally and financially.

We live with change every day; it's in everything we do. While the alarm is probably set for the same time every morning, some days we jump out of bed and on others we hit the snooze button. Our routines and habits can also be impacted by things outside our control, such as heavy traffic or our favourite café running out of organic activated almond milk.

CHANGE CATALYSTS

A catalyst is something that causes a change in something else. It can be as simple as a change in temperature that makes a cake rise or something more complex, such as our hormones. Dopamine, oxytocin and endorphins make us feel good and happy, and our body produces cortisol when we are stressed to engage the "fight or flight" response.

Change can result from external or internal factors, which directly affect how receptive we are to them. The difference is how much time we have to process the change, and how much control we have in the "when, where and how" of making it. If the change is something we decided we needed to do to make our lives better, then we are likely to have processed the thinking over a period of time before becoming committed to making it a success. However, if the change is externally imposed, then it may take our minds some time to process what this means for us.

Some catalysts, like losing a job, are so significant that they demand change right away, while others build up over time and eventually trigger an action when the cumulative pressure becomes too much, like a bad relationship.

Catalysts for change can fall into several categories, including:

Blindsiders: These are things we don't see in advance, like the bus in the movie *Speed* coming out of nowhere and slamming into a car. They can be either positive (winning the lottery) or negative (you're fired!). Blindsiders may be unexpected, however just because we didn't see them coming doesn't mean they weren't obvious to others. Like a broken relationship, often we miss the signs because we're in avoidance mode and didn't want to see them but when we tell our friends they may act unsurprised.

Forecasters: Just like a weather forecast, sometimes we get advance signs or notice. When we expect a storm and see the blackening skies, we can take the appropriate action to close windows. In many cases, such as AI and COVID-19, the catalyst may not cause job losses immediately. We were able to see the signs and anticipate the impact of evolving AI capabilities or COVID closing borders, adapting where we could. The consequences might not change, but we have time to prepare ourselves mentally and physically so we can start to take action in advance.

Pressure cookers: Have you ever lost it with someone in a way that seems disproportionate to the event? I am guilty of the odd bit of "contained" road rage. As I drive along the freeway on my way to work, one slow driver hogging the fast lane will be a slight annoyance. However, if I keep getting held up by slow drivers, my level of frustration builds and builds until I'm a red-faced cranky driver ready to explode. The same can happen in all aspects of our lives. Small, insignificant stuff can build up and build up until we can't take it anymore and we explode into action, demanding change.

Ostrich: Sometimes we may decide the catalyst is too confronting and it's easier to bury our head in the sand and pretend nothing is changing, in other words be like an ostrich. This catalyst involves quitting, and by giving up we leave the door open for impending change to occur. The ostrich can be a secondary response to blindsiders, forecasters and pressure cookers. Although we don't want it to happen, our inaction means that we don't proactively deter or stop the change from happening. We inadvertently invite it into our lives. Not paying debts and avoiding the resulting demand letters is an example of the ostrich who pretends that bankruptcy court is not part of their foreseeable future. Avoidance can also be a response to something huge that blindsides us, like a devastating health diagnosis.

Thrillseekers: A thrillseeker actively goes looking for change and excitement. They have become addicted to the adrenaline that comes with uncertainty and seeing how things play out. A thrillseeker will often instigate change just to mix things up. They get a strange sense of reward from being able to manage change while everyone else is fighting it. Such people tend to be entrepreneurs, innovators, job hoppers, commitment-phobes and rule breakers.

CATEGORY	RESPONSE TO CHANGE
Blindsiders	Shock, disbelief, anger, frustration
Forecasters	Acceptance, albeit reluctant
Pressure cookers	Overreaction, often out of proportion
Ostrich	Avoidance, ignorance and disbelief
Thrillseekers	Looking for change, challenge or innovation

While each catalyst can occur independently, they sometimes overlap. For example, a breast cancer nurse shared how all too often she sees patients come in with very obvious lumps in their breasts. As she points out, the lumps are so obvious that it's clear the person has known about them for quite a while, but has been avoiding it, hoping it wasn't true. Their unwillingness to accept the reality of the situation (ostrich) and take action when they first noticed it (blindsider) resulted in a much worse prognosis. The stress of this could then cause them to overreact to other things happening in their lives (pressure cooker) and throw caution to the wind and look to change the things they had been putting up with for way too long (thrillseeker).

When I was fortunate to study at Harvard University, other than tragically re-enacting scenes from the movie *Legally Blonde*, I learned a saying from a professor that has stuck with me. He said: "Bad news is like owing taxes. You either pay now, or you pay later with penalties plus interest. But you will pay!"

WHAT WERE YOU THINKING?

This is probably a good time to introduce you to *Bob*, the star of my last book, *Sort Your Sh!t Out*. We use our senses, sight, touch, smell, hearing and taste, to monitor and take in the world around us. But it's our minds that process all this incoming data to understand what it means for us. I call my mind *Bob*, because it's useful to have some objectivity to separate fact from fiction.

Bob is a master of fake news because, like an overprotective parent, he will do anything to keep me from getting hurt, physically or emotionally. If I felt abandoned as a child, *Bob* may create a story that I can't trust anyone so that I don't go through that negative experience again.

Think about the stories *your Bob* tells you that aren't true. Often when I'm between consulting contracts, *Bob* will start to instil self-doubt by suggesting that maybe I won't get the next gig or that I'm not good enough. He may try to convince you that without the title of pilot or CEO, you are nothing, a failure. To help keep your mind in check I suggest giving it a name. My wife calls hers Frau, as it criticises her constantly with German efficiency. Her daughter calls hers Miranda Priestly, after the ruthless character played by Meryl Streep in the movie *The Devil Wears Prada*.

While I named *Bob* after the character in the series *Blackadder*, I only recently realised that *Bob* also stands for Boss of Brain. Think about the power of the mind. Someone suffering from anorexia will overrule their body's need for fuel because of their brain's overwhelming belief that they are fat. In some cultures, when a witch doctor casts a spell, people are known to die simply because they believe they will. When we talk about reinvention, we need to ensure our minds don't sabotage our efforts through procrastination, fear of failure, or any one of the thousands of other reasons *Bob* will roll out to avoid the change because change brings with it uncertainty.

One of *Bob*'s biggest fears is seeing us fail. If you've lost your job, *Bob* may try to panic you by telling you that you're unlikely to find a similar job, or even that you'll be unemployed forever. Or if your relationship status is about to become "single", *Bob* could whisper that you'll be alone for the rest of your life. Being able to distinguish between reality and what we believe is real is a very powerful skill and calling "BS" on *Bob* when he's running out of control can help us avoid being debilitated by the uncertainty we face. *Bob* will often try to convince us to take control of every aspect of our lives and avoid the things that we can't control. This is why we eagerly embrace the changes we initiate and try to swerve those that are imposed externally.

Below is a list of the top stressors identified in the Holmes and Rahe Stress Scale, a tool developed by psychologists Thomas Homes and Richard Rahe in 1967 to measure the impact of common life events. As you read the list, you will note every one of them is a significant life change (mostly externally imposed) that brings with it high levels of uncertainty and significant consequences.

EVENT	IMPACT VALUE
Death of a spouse or partner	100
Divorce	73
Marital separation	65
Jail term	63
Personal injury	53
Marriage	50
Losing your job	47
Marital reconciliation	45
Retirement	45
Changes in family member's health	44
Pregnancy	40
Sex difficulties	39
Addition to family	39
Business readjustment	39
Changes in financial status	38

Interestingly, Christmas (12) and vacations (13) even make the list, albeit further down than some of the other big life events. Even good events bring with them stress and uncertainty. Reviewing the list, you will notice that each of these events demands changes to our identities. The related labels you used to describe yourself

STAGE 1: CHANGE

either internally or to the world will no longer be relevant. If you are divorced then your identity label goes from married to divorced. If you lose your job, your label become "unemployed", and so it goes throughout the list. The resulting changes in identity are a large part of why these events are so stressful.

Change influencers

When most of us hear the word influencers we think of those beautiful people living perfect lives oversharing their every thought, action and outfit with the world through their social media accounts. The role of influencers – regardless of whether they exist online or as part of our everyday life – is to highlight a path or lead the way for emerging trends and changes. Often it can be through them that our thoughts, actions, reactions and beliefs are shaped and influenced.

We all react differently when change comes knocking at our door. Personally, I get twitchy when things aren't regularly changing; I get bored when things remain too much the same. My definition of hell came true for me during COVID lockdown when we were stuck indoors, and I couldn't go out and interact with the world. Psychologists have expressed their concern about the short and long-term impacts of the pandemic lockdowns on people's mental wellbeing. It will be interesting to see how AI impacts our mental health over the next 5 to 10 years as our normal gets challenged and evolves. Some people used the lockdowns as an opportunity to learn something new, spend time with their family, and of course, bake sourdough bread. For others, it felt like too much space to be alone with their fears and issues without the freedom to escape using their usual distractions.

We all react differently to situations depending on our personality, outlook, experience and resilience. Some of us eagerly open the door and invite change in while others will double deadbolt the door and race around making sure all the windows are locked too. Unfortunately, change is pervasive and persistent; you can't simply lock the door and peek through the windows, hoping it's moved on to the neighbouring house without finding you. That isn't how the world works. Sure, you can try to avoid it, ignore it, abuse it and fight it with every ounce of your superhuman strength, but unless you can control the universe, time will continue to march on, and you will have to adapt or die. Not literally of course, but emotionally and professionally, or you will become a change-zombie with a mullet haircut stuck in purgatory between the new world and the non-existent past.

To avoid joining the unfashionable living dead, it's useful to understand some of the factors that influence the way *Bob* (aka your mind) is likely to react. Our reaction to change is dependent on a range of factors that can impact our emotional and psychological state.

Levels of stress: The more stress we are under, the more likely we are to overreact to a situation. If I've had an argument with my wife in the morning, I find there's a good chance I will overreact to the smallest thing at work, leaving me and my team wondering

WTF, where did that come from? Our stress levels build and build like Lego creations until they come tumbling down. One thing on its own, such as someone cutting in front of you in traffic, won't be enough to make you blow your top. But after the fourth or fifth time, the blood pressure is starting to rise. Like a traditional pressure cooker, things will keep building until it reaches a point where it needs to release. If you're super stressed, even the smallest change could cause you to blow your valve and lose it.

Degree of control: My mum died after a long battle with cancer and her final fight took months before she finally had enough. Our family had time to adjust and come to terms with our impending loss. Mum helped us deal with many of our emotions in advance and, although we were devastated when she took her final breath, there was also a sense of relief that she was no longer in pain. Not long after this, my aunty unexpectedly died from a heart attack, and I realised how fortunate we were to be able to say goodbye and mentally prepare for a life without Mum. The same advance planning happens when you decide to resign or retire rather than being fired or made redundant. Both require emotional and financial adjustments, but the unexpected change is more likely to set *Bob* off on a frenzy of anger, self-doubt, anxiety and possibly even depression.

Threat to identity: *Bob* loves to be able to brag and if you have (or had) a title that commands respect, he will be desperate to hang onto it. If *Bob* believes that we had or deserve a higher level of respect or status than we currently have, he will make this the focus of all our thoughts. For the suddenly unemployed this change in identity can be a significant struggle and adjustment to make to avoid sinking into a dark place. If you have just gone through a relationship breakdown, regardless of who called it quits, you become hyper-conscious that you are now single. Going to restaurants or cinemas alone is many people's nightmare, as their paranoid *Bob* starts thinking that everyone is judging them. Personally, I have been able to tame my *Bob* on this point and now love going to restaurants alone because I don't have to share desserts or choose a dish my wife and I both like!

Scale of change: If I go to my favourite café and they tell me they're out of almond milk for my mocha (don't judge), I'll probably decide to go with cow's milk or maybe a frappé (OK, now you can judge). If the event is life-changing, like unexpectedly finding yourself single, then it's likely to demand *Bob's* focus, often becoming all-consuming. These are the times when *Bob* needs to be kept in check. He often starts spouting fake news as he blows everything out of proportion. For example, while losing a job is traumatic, it also provides opportunities to explore other career options. Given the scale of changes AI is expected to bring, this is why it may seem so daunting.

Impact (real or perceived): How much the change impacts our "normal" lives influences how much attention we pay to the event. Take a mobile phone off a 16-year-old for the weekend to see the impact of a life-changing event. Forty-eight hours without our phones would test many of us regardless of age, but for a teenager this is their contact with their social network. The real impact is insignificant in the real world, but in the head of the disconnected teen it's likely to be perceived as the "end of the world". Perception is reality as far as *Bob* is concerned. *Bob* doesn't like surprises, so with any change he will make a quick call on how much it will impact us. The more significant the impact, the more anxious he will become and start setting off alarms. Importantly for our stress levels, it doesn't matter whether *Bob* is right or wrong at this point, because *Bob*'s perception influences our reality and if he believes it to be true, as far as we are concerned, it *is* true. *Bob* is the master magician, manipulating our perspective to create fake news to encourage us to keep things the same.

Previous experience: Like anything in life if you've gone through something similar before, *Bob* has reference points to let him know it will all be OK. The more often we do something, the more confident we become in our ability to deal with the situation: it's called self-efficacy. In pilot training you learn to crash a plane safely, or at least simulate the actions. One routine is called "stalling the plane". You pull back on the controls, flying the plane upwards until gravity stops you climbing, then the plane stalls and you start falling out of the sky towards your impending death. If that isn't harrowing enough, you're never really sure whether it will fall to the left or the right, which requires you to react differently depending on the fall.

Hopefully when you do this the first time your instructor is beside you, helping you recover and level off the plane. Stalls are an integral part of learning to fly and something you practise over and over again so that if you're faced with the real thing, you react appropriately and don't literally fall out of the sky. *Bob* is a little lazy, so when we do the same things over and over again, he sets up neural pathways in the brain so that the actions become a habit and run on automatic pilot.

I've been unemployed before, sometimes by my choice and sometimes not, and as a consultant there are spells where gigs just dry up. If you've been unemployed before, then you will probably do the things that worked for you last time and use the lessons you learned to improve the things that didn't work out. If you haven't been through similar situations, then *Bob* will be more likely to hit the panic button to prepare you for a range of possibilities. But the longer the situation continues, the louder *Bob*'s voice becomes until it seems like he's using a megaphone to bark all your insecurities and anxieties at you. If you're like me, the longer it is between similar situations, the more anxious you become, because you've lost touch with what worked last time. You probably wouldn't want to fly with me if I hadn't been in a plane for some years – in fact, I wouldn't want to be there without an instructor either.

Flexibility: As someone who has had 43 jobs, I like to think I'm pretty adaptable. I can apply the skills I've learned from one job to another. My days as a teacher have served me well in nearly every job I've had since. I can present to large groups and understand how learning new skills involves levels of uncertainty and fear. This adaptability affords me options to leverage if I ever find myself looking for my next gig to add to the list. Flexibility is the ability to explore options and refocus when the need or opportunity arises; resilience is the trait that determines whether you can keep going when things are looking grim and whether you can tell *Bob* to STFU (shut the fuck up) when he's trying to convince you that things are completely hopeless and you should quit. We'll talk about the critical element of resilience in more detail later on.

Mindset: Some people are just so damn positive, you want to "accidentally" spill coffee on them. These Positive Petes seem to be able to find something to love in the worst of situations. House burned down? No problem, I didn't like the colour of the carpet anyway, they may say. There is such thing as toxic positivity though, where someone is so positive that they don't take steps to manage the situation. Then there are the Negative Nellys. If you tell them, "Congratulations, you've won the lottery", they'll respond, "Oh great, now I'll have all the relatives hitting me up for a loan". Many self-help books talk about how positive affirmations can keep us upbeat. Unfortunately, they didn't work for me and *Bob*'s anxieties and self-doubt. For me it was the equivalent of giving a termite-infested house a new coat of paint. Sure, it looks good for a little while, but eventually you're going to have to deal with the real problems, not just gloss over them, before it all falls down around you.

In her bestselling book *Mindset*, Carol Dweck identifies two types of mindsets: a "fixed" mindset or a "growth" mindset. The category we fall into is a major determinant of whether or not we succeed. People with fixed mindsets believe their intelligence or ability is set in stone – and their *Bob* cares a lot about looking smart. When *Bob* is in control the fixed mindset people will "avoid challenges (because they might lead to failure), give up easily (because setbacks might hurt their self-image), and see hard work and effort as a waste, because they think they're either talented enough to do something or they're not," Dweck writes.

Those of us with a growth mindset see our intelligence as changeable and ever-evolving. They are in control of *Bob* and see their minds as something that can "be developed, and they have an intense desire to learn. They embrace challenges, persist against setbacks, and see hard work as a chance to get better at something," Dweck explains. Our mindset determines how we receive news about change and if we pick ourselves up and get on with dealing with the resulting situation.

What's at stake: The more important the outcome is to us, the greater the expectation, and correspondingly, the more pressure *Bob* puts on us to succeed. Just like the impact of the event, expectations are often based on *Bob*'s fake news. He may have created expectations that are unrealistic or totally blown out of proportion, like losing your job and despairing that you will never find your dream career ever again. The bigger *Bob* builds up the pressure, the greater the fall. And the longer we may end up wallowing in the setback.

Bob is a pretty simple guy. He sees unmet expectations as failures and will try to convince us that we either failed or that they didn't matter in the first place. *Bob* also has trouble distinguishing between unrealistic expectations or long shots and realistic outcomes. For example, have you ever noticed that you feel disappointed when you didn't win the $20 million jackpot despite it being a *billion* to one that you would have the winning numbers? Often, the biggest challenges are not the hurdles and obstacles the world will present you with, but rather the imaginary ones you create for yourself. The monsters we create in our head are often much bigger, badder and scarier than those we encounter in the real world.

Bob likes where he is right now because this is what he knows. He has been able to build a plethora of habits, thought patterns, behaviours and routines to make the best of *this* situation. He will use every one of your fears and phobias to convince you that where you are heading is not worth the effort and could make you look foolish.

As the actor Jim Carrey said: "Life opens up opportunities to you, and you either take them or you stay afraid of taking them."

STAGE 1: CHANGE

AI – A generational change

I was initially reluctant to include a chapter on AI in a book about reinvention. Afterall, even before I finish writing this chapter the AI landscape will have evolved and changed again beyond what I could have only dreamed of. By the time you are reading this book even more changes will be becoming obvious and the impacts for all of us are likely to be making our heads spin.

Change is one of the few constants in human history. From the dawn of civilisation to the age of technology, we've seen revolutions that have altered the course of societies, economies, and personal lives. But there is no avoiding it. The AI genie has been let out of the bottle and no matter how much we dislike it there is no putting the stopper back in. The reality is that we, as a society, are living through one of the most significant and rapid changes in the history of humanity. Sure, at an individual level, there are events which could change our lives more rapidly, such as winning lotto, natural disasters, health diagnoses or accidents. But for humanity AI is the once-in-a-generation change: the scale, speed, and depth of change we're experiencing today due to AI is unlike anything we've encountered before.

This wave of change is different, faster and more disruptive than previous ones, and we, as individuals, need to prepare for the personal reinvention required for us to stay relevant and hopefully thrive. For me personally, I am preparing myself for a huge change in my identity. I consider myself a pretty smart person and I believe I am someone who can get shit done. But the way I have succeeded at leveraging these talents will need to change. My job, my role in society, my perception of my place in the world around me, and therefore my identity, will all need to evolve.

Just like the industrial revolutions, the digital age, or even more subtle shifts like the advent of electricity, AI represents a profound change that will impact industries, jobs, and society at large. This transformation will be rapid, far-reaching, and deeply personal. Jobs we thought were secure may vanish or change drastically. Industries, and hence those involved with those industries will need to adapt – or risk being left behind. We are at a turning point in history, and understanding how these generational changes have played out previously can give us the tools to navigate the future.

The changes we face today – driven by AI – are unlike anything we've encountered before. It's not just about a shift in how we work or how we communicate. AI is about rethinking what it means to be human, what it means to have a job, and what it means to create, and even think and reason. The pace of change is accelerating, and we must evolve with it if we are to thrive or even just survive.

Historically, generational changes have always led to profound shifts in society, identity and therefore led to the need for people to reinvent themselves. I have excluded wars in this overview, but of course their resulting devastation and trauma will result in people needing to reinvent themselves and the same process applies. Here are a few key times in history where change was relatively swift, unexpected and transformative.

THE AGRICULTURAL REVOLUTION

Around 12,000 years ago, societies were primarily composed of hunter-gatherers. Survival was based on hunting animals and foraging for food. But then came the Agricultural Revolution, a period where humans began to domesticate plants and animals, leading to the first permanent settlements and the rise of civilisation. This shift fundamentally altered how people lived.

Agriculture allowed for the creation of surplus food, which in turn led to population growth, the development of cities, and the emergence of social hierarchies. However, not everyone was prepared for this change. Many early societies struggled with the shift, and those who adapted quickly were the ones that thrived. The agricultural revolution did not just change how humans interacted with the land: it reshaped the structure of society itself.

THE INDUSTRIAL REVOLUTION

Fast forward to the late 18th century and the Industrial Revolution marked another seismic shift. With the advent of machines, steam power and mass production, the world of work was transformed. Industries boomed, cities grew rapidly, and new technologies emerged at an unprecedented pace.

The work people had done for centuries such as agriculture, handcrafting goods and manual labour was suddenly replaced by factory jobs, powered by machines. Entire industries like textiles, coal mining and transportation were revolutionised. But with this change came a great deal of disruption. Entire jobs and crafts disappeared, and people who had once made a living by traditional methods now found themselves working in factories, sometimes under difficult conditions. The Industrial Revolution didn't just change the way people worked, it changed the way people saw themselves and their role in the world.

THE DIGITAL REVOLUTION

Then, in the late 20th century, came the Digital Revolution. The rise of personal computers, the internet, and digital communication transformed the global economy. The world became interconnected in ways that were previously unimaginable. The digital age created entirely new industries: software development, digital marketing, e-commerce, and more. But it also disrupted traditional industries. Print newspapers, for example, were gutted by the rise of digital media. Jobs that once required physical presence, such as bank tellers or travel agents, were replaced by online services. Again, society saw a rapid shift in how people worked, communicated and lived. Those who could adapt quickly and reinvent themselves in line with the change found new opportunities, while others struggled to keep up.

AI: THE NEXT GREAT GENERATIONAL CHANGE

Which brings us to the present where AI is poised to be the next great generational change. Much like the agricultural, industrial and digital revolutions before it, AI is not just a new tool – it's a new way of understanding the world. The rapid development of AI is altering how we interact with technology and each other, how industries operate, and how work is done. Machines are learning how to make decisions, process complex data, and even replicate certain aspects of human behaviour. AI is being implemented in healthcare, finance, transportation, retail and nearly every other sector you can think of.

But this time, the change is happening faster than ever before. Jobs that once seemed secure like drivers, accountants and customer service representatives are being transformed by automation. Entire industries are being restructured by AI. In the healthcare sector, for example, AI is improving diagnostic accuracy and patient care through machine learning. In finance, AI is predicting market trends and automating trading. In retail, AI is revolutionising supply chains and personalising customer experiences. While these advances present new opportunities, they also present challenges. Many jobs will be eliminated or drastically changed as AI takes over tasks once performed by humans, so we need to develop the skills to be adaptable and resilient to pivot to these new opportunities.

JOBS AND INDUSTRIES LIKELY TO BE IMPACTED BY AI

Here are some industries and jobs that are likely to experience significant change due to AI. On the positive side, from this seismic shift there will be opportunities and jobs that emerge in fields that probably don't even currently exist.

- **Transportation:** With the rise of self-driving vehicles, truck drivers, taxi drivers, and delivery personnel may find their jobs don't exist anymore or are drastically changed. However, new opportunities will emerge in the maintenance, programming, and oversight of autonomous vehicles.

- **Healthcare:** AI is already being used for diagnostics, administrative tasks, and even robotic surgeries. While some healthcare jobs may be replaced, AI will also create new roles, such as medical data analysts and health tech developers. There is a growing view that AI will help eradicate most human diseases and health conditions within the next decade.

- **Finance:** AI is revolutionising everything from algorithmic trading to fraud detection. While some banking jobs may be automated, new opportunities will emerge in areas like AI auditing, risk assessment and data analysis.

- **Retail and Customer Service:** AI-driven chatbots and automated checkout systems are already reshaping retail and customer service industries. Jobs in these fields may shift to roles focused on AI management and customer experience optimisation.

- **Knowledge industries:** AI is automating tasks in jobs such as consulting, project management, researcher law, journalism and marketing. Routine work like document review and content generation may be replaced, but new opportunities are likely to emerge in AI management, data analysis, and strategic decision-making roles.

- **Technology:** AI is reshaping software development, digital media, cybersecurity and IT management. While some technical roles may evolve or be automated, there will be increased demand for roles in AI development, machine learning engineering, and AI system integration.

POWER TO THE PEOPLE

It is important to note that it isn't all doom and gloom around AI. Change always brings with it opportunities and AI is likely to create industries and wealth from sources we have never thought of. It will also provide access to endless information and expertise allowing us to explore ideas and opportunities that had been previously out of reach, understanding or capabilities. A great example of this happened in 2023 when a mum got so frustrated after taking her sick son to over 17 specialist doctors with no satisfactory diagnosis, that she used ChatGPT to identify a likely cause and then worked with a new neurosurgeon to confirm the diagnosis. There was still a role for the human expertise, but AI was able to join the dots where humans were unable to.

I am loving exploring AI to see what I can create. Based on my adventures I have been able to create a board game called King of Dad Jokes, plan digital media strategies, create comprehensive feasibility studies for my countless business ideas and developed new recipes based on what I have in the fridge. I can build websites, do my own coding and be my own graphic designer and video creator too. I have also argued with ChatGPT when it has lied to me and learnt so much along the way. It is worth noting that, just like humans, the current versions of AI are known to "hallucinate", also commonly known as making shit up. It is getting better, but as at the end of 2024, AI still can misrepresent details to us and make mistakes. So just like in the real world, don't believe everything you read or are told by AI. I am loving having all this knowledge, creativity and power at my fingertips to explore, innovate and work more efficiently and cost effectively.

The rapid pace of these changes means that we must begin preparing to adapt now. The identity we hold in our current world, especially our roles in work and society, will demand we evolve quickly. The key to thriving in this environment is to embrace learning new skills, remain flexible, and be prepared for the shifts that are already happening. After all, just as AI is reinventing itself by learning and growing, we need to use this catalyst and do the same.

Why me? The emotions of change

When my mum died from cancer, I cycled through a range of emotions from anger to sadness, relief and depression. One of the most important people in my life had been taken away at the age of 61. When I was fired from my holiday job for being too distracted by the girls I worked with at the resort (I was 16 – no judgement, please), I remember feeling anger, sadness, self-doubt and depression, even though the job didn't mean that much to me.

In both these instances, I questioned, "Why me?"

When you list the emotions you experienced whenever you had to deal with a significant change in your life, you'll notice a pattern emerging. The pattern I've outlined above will probably sound similar to feelings you experienced in any life-changing event you went through.

Elisabeth Kübler-Ross, a Swiss psychologist, introduced her "five stages of dying" model to the world. It theorises that we go through denial, anger, bargaining, depression and acceptance in the face of death and other significant losses that cause grief. The model remains as relevant now as it did 50 years ago. The reason is that as humans, we become attached to people and things. When they're gone, we miss them. We may grieve for loved ones, missed opportunities, unwanted changes to routines and habits, a job, our identity – the list goes on.

If we were attached to anything that we no longer have in our lives, then it's likely we will experience grief in all its stages. Sometimes we have trouble recognising what it is we are grieving; we just know that something is broken or missing and we are experiencing some discomfort. During COVID I missed our family gatherings and real hugs instead having to make do with Zoom catch-ups peppered with "You're on mute, Dad".

Even if we are the instigator of the change, we're still likely to go through the stages of grief as we try to adapt to our new normal and let go of the past. We can even go through the stages of grief when we have moved on to something better, like a new job. We miss our previous normal and will grieve for the things that we have to let go.

To illustrate the five stages of the Kübler-Ross grief cycle, imagine you're watching the rose ceremony on *The Bachelor* (stop the fake indignation, we've all watched it at one time or another).

STAGE 1: CHANGE

Roses have been given out to most of the contestants and the last two are standing before the bachelor, anxiously awaiting the next name to be called. Will it be Sammy, squeezed into a sequined dress 17 sizes too small for her, or will it be tattooed Jojo, who looks like she might take out a contract on the bachelor if she doesn't get the rose?

Bachelor: Jojo, will you please accept this rose?

Jojo (looking smug, as if there was ever any doubt): Of course, Brad.

Camera pans from Jojo to Sammy, who looks like she's trying to make sense of what just happened.

Her immediate reaction is a little hard to figure out as the Botox and fillers do an excellent job of masking her emotions. She looks over at the posse of girls clutching their prized roses. She looks at the host and the bachelor, hopeful that they're hiding another rose somewhere. She can't believe what has just happened. Her **denial** is a natural response to such a public humiliation on national television. This is where her *Bob* tries to avoid the reality of what is happening, because it's a situation her *Bob* thinks she can't handle right now. Like Sammy, when confronted with a life-changing event like, say, losing our job, we may shut down emotionally or try to run away. The problem is the change is real and eventually we will have to deal with it. Unless we deal with it, our shit always seems to come to the surface, and it has this knack of coming out when we really don't want it to. In Sammy's case, she'll be able to watch this moment over and over again

63

once she gets home, similar to the scenarios *Bob* will often put on replay in our heads.

After the obligatory group hugs from the girl squad who are secretly celebrating her imminent departure, Sammy starts to get angry. The scene cuts to her as the look in her eyes goes from "Brad, I love you" to "You are dead to me". While the Botox may stop her face from showing the **anger**, her body language and words make it clear. Back in the real world, when we process life-changing news, we start to think about its impact on our lives: "What about the new house we just bought? Can I sell the $10,000 bike I've used only twice? How am I going to pay for the kids' schools? I love my life; I don't want it to change." Once we realise our loss is real, we're likely to become angry, irritable and anxious. During the post-dumping interview, Sammy starts to blame everyone for her demise. Brad didn't really get to know her; the other girls were mean to her; the producers set her up. While all three may be true, it's evidence that her *Bob* is looking for someone to blame, because someone else must be responsible for making her feel this way.

Back in the real world of unemployment, our *Bob*s are arguing, "If only my boss had been better at managing" or "This is the government's fault, why can't they see the harm this is doing?". Please forgive *Bob*, he's just trying to protect you by finding a way to shift the blame to someone else, just like he did for Sammy.

In the back of the limo as Sammy is whisked away from the remaining rose-endowed posse, she looks for ways to make her 15 minutes last longer. Maybe she can be the next bachelorette,

STAGE 1: CHANGE

or maybe she can create her own fitness YouTube channel. In his desperation to protect her from having to deal with her grief, *Bob* has begun **bargaining**. If you've lost your job, you might go back to your boss and suggest taking a pay cut, working three days a week or helping out in other areas. It may be completely illogical but at that point in time it may make complete sense to *Bob*. You may start looking to strike a deal with whichever gods you believe in, or even the ones you don't believe in. You might dive into a game of "what if" to try to bargain your way out of the situation. Depending on your mindset, this bargaining stage could be an act of desperation in trying to maintain the status quo (fixed mindset) or an act of exploration of the options for the next opportunity in line (growth mindset).

Make no mistake, such a public rejection will require a period of adjustment and perhaps one of **depression**, which means tubs of Ben & Jerry's Triple Caramel Chunk ice cream, more tissues than are now acceptable post the COVID toilet paper run of 2020, and reruns of *Sex and the City*. It's now been a week since that fateful announcement, and you and Sammy are struggling to find the energy or motivation to do anything. Giving up and binge eating while watching Netflix or endless TikTok dance moves seems like the most sensible thing to do now. *Bob* is trying to avoid any further hurt, so he convinces you that the best thing you can do is sit around and feel sorry for yourself – after all, you've just been through something pretty traumatic. Even though it's unhealthy, *Bob* would prefer you stayed here because at least this is a situation that won't hurt you any further; avoiding the big bad world out there makes sense, he argues. How long this state lasts will vary – many people will move forward while still coming to terms with their loss, while for others this stage could last the rest of their lives and leave them debilitated.

After a period of time, hopefully, things start to return to normal as you start accepting the change. For Sammy, **acceptance** means getting back into her routine of HIIT classes and activewear selfies; if you've lost your job, you might start thinking about the next steps. You begin to feel a sense of normality again. Of course, it can never be the normal you once had, because that is no longer and only exists in our memories of the past. At this stage we start to accept our new reality and make the necessary adjustments to function in this new world. Sammy is dating a football player who slid into her DMs and she's accepted a non-speaking role in a film student's short film. We may tidy the house, get out of our pyjamas for the first time in a week, and start reaching out to contacts to explore new opportunities. Acceptance doesn't mean we have forgotten the past, just that *Bob* has come to terms with us moving forward to create our new future. It's at this point we will consciously make the decision about whether we proactively take control of the next steps or remain a victim and wait to see what happens.

Whenever we lose something we value, grief is unavoidable, and despite our best efforts to bottle it up, avoid or ignore it, we will eventually have to deal with it. To create a new path, we must first acknowledge and respect the past that has brought us to this point and give ourselves permission to grieve for what has been lost, so we can focus our attention on the opportunities that lie before us.

STAGE 1: CHANGE

As Sammy says in her activewear post: "#Grief is like a box of chocolates: once you start you can't stop, but eventually it's time to take a deep breath, close the box and step into summer ready to rock the latest bikini!"

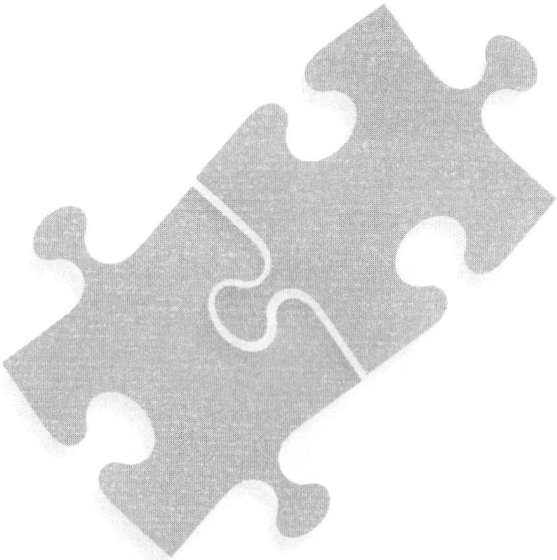

Stage 2: Reality Check

"Reality is merely an illusion, albeit a very persistent one".

— Albert Einstein

losing control

At Movie World on the Gold Coast, a roller-coaster is advertised as the "tallest, longest and fastest ride in the Southern Hemisphere". In a sad attempt to be the super cool uncle, I lined up with my nieces for 20 minutes along with a hundred other fearless uncles and kids to experience the thrills on offer. On the inside, my *Bob* was having an anxious internal conversation about my likelihood of throwing up or breaking into tears when they take the always-embarrassing mid-ride photo. I kept reminding myself, "You MUST be the cool uncle!".

Roller-coasters are all about control, or the lack thereof. You have little choice but to give yourself over to the experience of spinning, falling and being thrown around like a rag doll. If your fear or need to stay in control takes over and makes your *Bob* decide to try to fight the ride, there's a good chance you'll hurt yourself while rocketing around at 115 kilometres an hour.

If you're a true roller-coaster aficionado, you know the only way to ride something this big is to close your eyes, throw your arms up in the air and submit to the experience. For some of us, the mere thought of lining up would send us into a sweat and end with us faking a heart attack to get out of such nonsense.

Fighting life's ups and downs is about as useless as trying to get off the roller-coaster once it's started (you can't). Trying to control the world and outside factors is often a waste of effort. One of the main differences between control freaks and those going with the flow, other than their anxiety levels, is the ability to remain calm and comfortable with uncertainty.

Bob hates uncertainty because it increases our chances of failure. *Bob* knows that failure opens us up to feelings of inadequacy and long-term low self-confidence and self-worth issues, so he'll do whatever he can to avoid us experiencing that pain. *Bob* may use confidence – real or fake – as a guide to managing uncertainty. In surveys, public speaking consistently ranks as one of our greatest fears, even greater than sharks, indicating how much power the fear of failure has over us.

To illustrate the power of control, imagine you're experiencing one of the following situations.

STAGE 2: REALITY CHECK

SCENARIO	WHO IS IN CONTROL — YOU	WHO IS IN CONTROL — SOMEONE ELSE	RESPONSE SCENARIOS — YOU	RESPONSE SCENARIOS — SOMEONE ELSE
SEPARATION	You decide the relationship isn't working anymore. After trying to make it work, you tell your partner you're leaving them.	Your partner decides the relationship isn't working anymore. They tell you they're leaving.	You and your partner separate. After a period of adjustment, you set up your Tinder account. Remember three hours after a break-up is too soon.	You and your partner separate. After a period of adjustment, you get a cat and stalk your ex on Facebook. Remember three years of pining is too long; just set up the Tinder account.
MEETING SOMEONE ELSE	You meet someone online and feel a real connection. You decide to tell your partner before it goes any further.	Your partner meets someone online. They decide to tell you before it goes any further.	You hope you and your partner can work out what was wrong in the relationship and that they can forgive you.	After you've used their toothbrush to clean the toilet you and your partner try to work out what was wrong in the relationship and you try to forgive them.
LEAVING YOUR JOB	You resign from your job. You're over it and you want to explore other options.	Your boss tells you that your job no longer exists and you should explore your options.	You are free to explore options and start a side gig breeding racing pigeons and working at KFC. You have never been happier.	After you have used their toothbrush to clean the toilet, you eventually realise that your boss was weird and you're better off being free to explore options.
RELOCATION	You get offered a great new job but it means you will have to move to the country for the promotion.	Your partner gets offered a great new job but it means you will have to move to the country.	You move to take up the new job and have never been happier. Who would have thought you could combine pigeon racing and KFC for the ideal life?	After you have used their toothbrush to clean the toilet and ever so briefly consider options 1 and 2 above, you move to support your partner and wonder how long it takes to bake a pigeon.

Control allows you to take charge of the variables that come your way and become the master of your destiny. From your captain's chair, you're able to direct when you would prefer changes to happen and prepare yourself for the inevitable adjustments you will need to make. The change will be made very much on your terms.

SPHERE OF CONTROL

Bob loves certainty, and therefore control, because this brings predictability and eliminates surprises. He can use the habits and routines he has so carefully constructed to manage all aspects of our lives to protect us. Unfortunately for *Bob*, we can't control the things happening outside our direct sphere of influence or control. If something is within our control, we are often able to design and manage the outcome to meet our expectations. However, when things fall outside our control, then where it lies in our sphere of influence determines how likely it is we will get what we want or even close to it. If our influence is high, then we can shape the outcome. But if we have little or no influence, we could end up having to just accept what comes our way.

STAGE 2: REALITY CHECK

DISINTERESTED

INTEREST

CONCERN

INFLUENCE

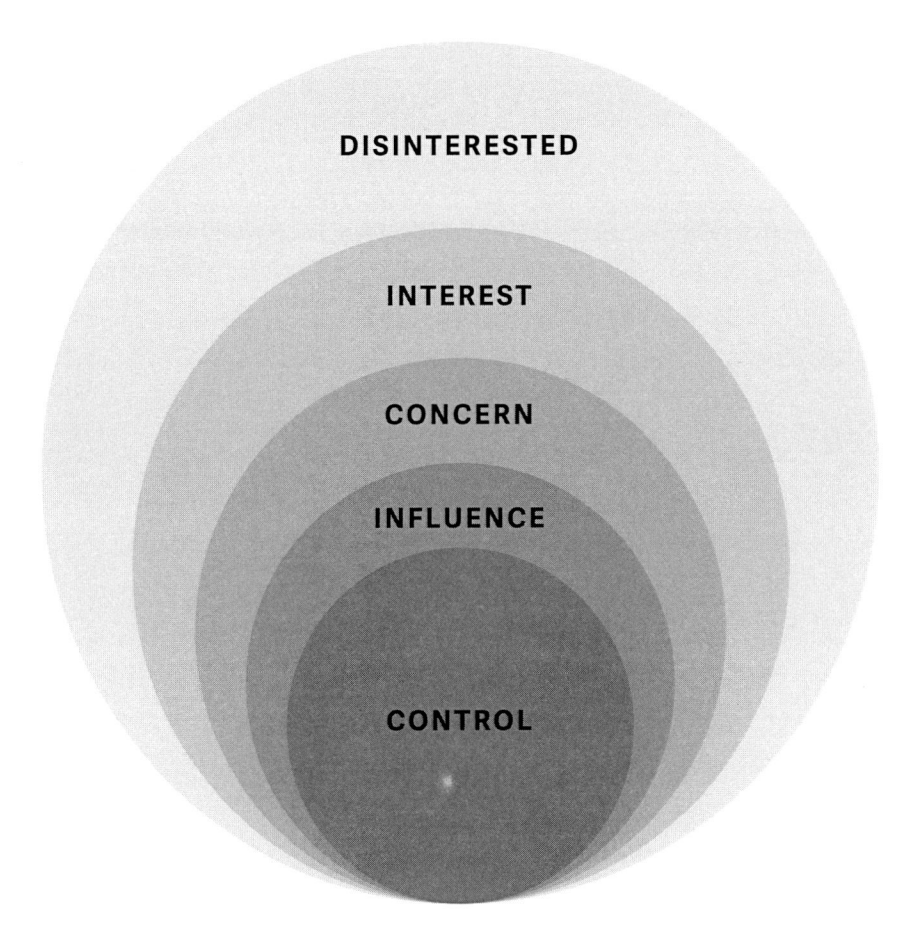

CONTROL

Spheres of control

Given *Bob* is a control freak, he's likely to need a period of adjustment to come to terms with not getting his way. Our sphere of control is usually those things directly related to us. We can control what time we wake up, what we eat, what we're interested in – the list goes on. But as soon as other factors start to come into our world, like whether my wife will like my choice of entrée, you move into the sphere of influence. Whether I get to have the scallops or the soup will depend on my degree of influence and of course, what my wife wants. As we move outside our circles of control and influence we enter into the world of concern, where we are active observers – like choosing a new colour for the bedroom. I am part of the decision-making process, and it's strange how often my choice eventually is exactly the same as my wife's. Beyond concern lies the sphere of interest, where I have very little say or stakes in the outcome, but I'm interested to see what happens. For example, did Sammy and the football player work out? Outside of the sphere of interest lies a barren land called the sphere of disinterest, which is filled with...well, let's be honest, who cares? If we did, it would be in our sphere of interest.

The importance of the sphere of control model is that it highlights where we should focus our energy. Trying to control things that are beyond our control is just a waste of energy and we should really focus our attention on the things we can control and influence.

STAGE 2: REALITY CHECK

This too shall pass

Legend has it that King Solomon charged his wise men with creating a ring that would comfort him in dark times. After much consideration they returned with a ring etched with the words "This too shall pass", and whenever he felt down, anxious or depressed he was to look at the ring and remind himself that what he was feeling was only a point in time and not destined to last forever. While I can't confirm the accuracy of the tale, I can attest to the usefulness of this phrase. When my relationships have broken down, when I find myself between gigs, when my expectations aren't met, when I feel like I have failed, I have recalled this phrase and it seems to bring things back into context.

Life-changing events, regardless of whether they are good or bad for us, always cause a degree of disruption to *Bob*'s cherished normality. The greater the disruption and the less control we have over the change, the more stressed and anxious we become. Remember, *Bob* is a control freak who can set you on a dark path when he encounters unwanted change. The problem is that as Buddha once said, "Nothing is forever, except change". Given the wisdom of Buddha, I would suggest that *Bob* is screwed if he plans to resist change.

But that's exactly what he does. He likes consistency and predictability and generally dislikes surprises. Obviously, he loves gifts and things that make him feel valued, loved and secure, because they really don't demand significant changes. Most of the time, these cool things enhance our lives and give us a buzz, which is something *Bob* loves. But when they start to threaten elements of the foundation of our lives, then the anxiety, stress, fear and depression ratings start to go off the scale.

The problem with being in a stressed state is that we end up with a rush of adrenaline through our bodies. This prepares us to physically respond to the stressful situation. Traditionally, the two responses that we are preparing for are fight or flight. If I'm in an old, spooky house and the lights go out and a door slams, the ancient reptilian part of my brain prepares my body to either run away or fight whatever ghoul comes my way. Now, I'm going to be honest here: I'm not going into the basement or the attic to search for the fuse box, I'm running or hiding. This is where I believe the third response comes into the picture: hiding or freezing. We may use hiding as a strategy to avoid having to fight or flight.

Back in the Scooby Doo haunted house you'll find me hiding behind the couch, holding my breath and my hands over my eyes, while maintaining my masculinity, of course. The debilitating aspect of freezing is that our mind is overcome with fear and is trying to process the information. In the animal kingdom, it's the equivalent of playing dead.

The problem with a strategy of hiding or avoidance is that at some point you're going to have to move. If you leave your move too late you can become more exposed as the world you were used to moves on. Avoidance, while useful when faced with a bus coming towards you, is not so helpful after you've been hit by it. Avoidance of immediate threats is a strategy you should seriously consider where possible, however, avoidance of reality or avoidance of dealing with the consequences of a life-changing event after it has happened is less than ideal.

Ignoring the lump in your breast, staying in a dysfunctional relationship that stopped working for you long ago, ignoring AI, or sitting at home waiting for the phone to ring and hoping your job will magically reappear are all examples of avoidance. It's *Bob's* way of resisting the reality that you need to change and do things differently. *Bob* is hanging on to the hope that if you avoid the situation he won't have to deal with it. But as we know from any Stephen King horror story, the things we fear the most always end up finding us hiding behind the couch and forcing us to confront them.

To summarise: our options in response to stress and anxiety include running, fighting back or hiding. Depending on the situation the correct response will vary. But the key is to have a plan, know your strengths and weaknesses, and stay alert rather than shut down.

LEARNING TO ADAPT

Stress is not only a state of mind but also our physiological response to situations and activities. As a gym instructor I would train people to achieve their physical goals by putting their bodies under stress. The more you push yourself, the more your body has to react to the additional work. If the stress is lifting weights, your muscles will start to grow to physiologically adapt to the new world of having to move heavier weights. If you want to learn something new, like playing the guitar, you're putting your brain and fingers under stress. Over time both will adapt, and instead of having to watch the strings and wear bandaids on your bleeding fingers, you'll be able to play your favourite song with your eyes closed.

Bob adapts to the things we do regularly by creating habits or routines that we can do without thinking. In our brains these are neural pathways, which, like our muscles, strengthen the more we use them. These pathways are for stresses or activities that we are familiar with; however, things become more interesting when the stress or risk is something we don't deal with regularly. When *Bob* doesn't have a strong reference point, or there isn't any at all for the situation you're dealing with, he may become overwhelmed, reverting to anxiety and depression as his fallback position as he tries to recalibrate.

Bob sometimes lives in the past, longing for the way things used to be, or in the future, focused on what needs to be done to achieve a goal. Or he might be present, where he appreciates what's happening in the here and now. Some of us focus too much on the things that have passed, which we can't change, or the things in the future, which may never eventuate, rather than the things we can control, which is the here and now.

The longer things go on the more *Bob* adjusts his expectations and starts to convince you that you are deserving of the life you are living, for better or for worse. Often at this stage you start to plan your future based on things staying the same or getting better. The memories of any difficulties or challenges of the past start to fade into the history chronicles. Even the smallest things that are associated with this life become part of our entitlement.

Like me hiding behind the couch in the haunted house, *Bob* is trying to figure out what the next steps are. Like Sammy going through her grief cycle, *Bob* needs a period of time to adjust and to grieve for the loss of his previous normal. But the longer he continues focusing on the past and what has been lost, the deeper the depression and the longer the negativity and darkness is likely to last. *Bob* may play the scenarios over and over again like a broken record (remember those?), which can build up neural pathways of negativity that need to be disrupted.

When that happens, call on your inner King Solomon and tell *Bob* that this too shall pass. And if that doesn't work, pull out the big guns and tell him to STFU. The recognition that your current state of being is only a point in time and the future is yet to play out, and therefore there are endless options that could change your fortunes, may just be enough to start you on the path to action rather than hiding in the darkness, eating donuts and trying to avoid your butt flesh becoming meshed into the fabric of the lounge.

The good, the bad and the ugly

The Good, the Bad and the Ugly is the title of the 1966 spaghetti western movie that made Clint Eastwood a star, and it's also the name of a process I came across when I was working in the fashion industry. My ex-wife Julie and I had a fashion business that manufactured, wholesaled and retailed clothing around Australia and internationally. The world of fashion is about forecasting the next trend and then manufacturing the designs that will hopefully be the next big thing. The problem with fashion is that often you're designing six to twelve months in advance, investing in the future without the aid of a crystal ball.

To maximise their success, retailers review the winners, losers and *meh!* designs each season to help inform ongoing purchasing decisions by determining what to do more of (the good), what to improve on (the bad), and what to avoid (the ugly) – nicknamed a GBU. The GBU review process is integral to maintaining a high-performance business. It's about learning from the past and focusing efforts on the things that are working and have potential and letting go of the stuff that isn't working.

The GBU process applies to our personal lives as much as it does to fashion businesses. It also makes me approach reviewing my life with a bit more swagger, as my *Bob* imagines I'm one of the gun-toting characters on the silver screen. Of course, in this scenario I'm always one of the good guys focused on eliminating the bad elements and turning around those qualities that should or need to be saved with a bit of tweaking here and there.

While this can be a personal review of yourself, it's also worth doing a 360-degree or all-round review. Because *Bob* wants to protect you, he's prone to telling you a lie here and there. To avoid the fake news that *Bob* may be telling you to convince you that you don't need to change, you should also get input from others who know you in relation to the life event. The aim of completing a GBU is to help you come through this opportunity for improvement with considerably less shit than you brought into this situation.

The Johari window is a great model that can help you understand how your *Bob* can taint your honest personal review. The Johari window is a psychology tool that compares what we believe to be true about ourselves and what others believe to be true about us. It's important to understand that just because we believe something to be true doesn't necessarily make it so. I often fall into the trap of believing I possess a degree of coolness because I listen to rap music, only to be brought back to earth by my nephews, wife, friends and unknown strangers, who remind me very bluntly that I have no street cred at all.

	KNOWN TO SELF	**NOT KNOWN TO SELF**
KNOWN TO OTHERS	**Captain Obvious** Things everyone knows	**Captain Oblivious** Things others know that you don't
UNKNOWN TO OTHERS	**Hidden secrets** Stuff only you know	**Unknown** Who cares because no one knows

The *Mastering the Art of Reinvention* version of the Johari window

The Johari window allows us to see a more complete picture: within all this feedback lies the truth.

When I was fired from my recreational camp job as a teenager I was more than a little miffed because I honestly thought I was doing a good job (captain oblivious), despite my manager noticing that the place was often a shambles. After all, I never missed a shift, as we all knew (captain obvious). I blamed the workload, however, when they replaced me with someone who kept everything nicely organised, it made *Bob* realise the workload wasn't the problem. I thought my role was to keep customers happy and be a social butterfly, which probably stemmed from wanting to be liked (hidden secrets), but my new unemployed status seemed to indicate otherwise. At that point I had no idea I would go on to another 42 gigs – and neither did they (unknown).

Similarly, if you were made redundant from your job while others were selected to stay on then maybe there was a reason that you haven't considered. Likewise, if your relationship broke down, it's more than likely that you also had a part to play in its demise. Whatever the event, try to understand what led to this change and what you need to do differently.

You should quiz not only your friends, but those who will tell you the cold harsh truth, and if possible, your ex, boss or whoever played a part in the event to understand your role in the breakdown. Of course, you could choose not to dig into the reasons for your life-changing event, which means you're content being where you are and *Bob* has succeeded in convincing you that being unhappy or dissatisfied is better than facing the risk that comes with change. But remember that choosing to do nothing is still a decision you have made.

Below is a table to help you take stock of what part you played to get to this point in your life. It covers what traits haven't served you well and you should leave behind; what traits that are worth maintaining; and the traits you should work on to improve.

MASTERING THE ART OF REINVENTION

TRAITS	GOOD What's working for you that you don't want to lose?	BAD What could you improve on that would help you achieve your goal?	UGLY What do you need to stop doing and/or let go of?
Mindset: are you a positive or negative person (fixed or growth mindset)?			
Preferences and choices			
Personality			
Ego			
Values			
Skills			
Priorities			
Titles			
Tasks			
Distractions			
Loved ones – how you treat them			
Loved ones – how they treat you			

STAGE 2: REALITY CHECK

In our attempt to cleanse, we could benefit from some of the wisdom espoused by Japanese tidying and organising expert Marie Kondo and her KonMari Method. While this method is normally applied to tidying one's living areas, it transcends into tidying one's life as an added benefit. You're probably thinking things are starting to get a bit weird, but hang in there. The steps involved in the KonMari Method are:

Commit yourself to tidying up: If we're not committed to making a change, then when the going gets tough and we have to make some hard decisions we'll probably avoid them. So decide whether you're all in or not. Either option is fine because ultimately it's your decision and your life. But if you are desperately unhappy where you are, you need to tell *Bob* to STFU and get on with it.

Imagine your ideal lifestyle: Goal setting is something we'll discuss in more detail later in the book, but at this point it's worthwhile taking time to visualise what you want your life to look like. COVID made many of us revaluate what's important to us and how we want to live. For instance, many people traded inner-city apartments for rural or regional living, and workplaces now have greater acceptance of work-from-home arrangements, allowing people to design a lifestyle they love. This step is not about planning the accumulation of possessions, but about identifying what a meaningful life looks like to you and who you want to be.

Finish discarding first: Before getting rid of items, sincerely thank each item for serving its purpose. I really like this step, because all too often *Bob* likes to beat us up and hang on to shit (beliefs, failures and habits, for example) that should be discarded. I get

87

that thanking your beliefs before letting them go could seem a bit out there. But think about it: everything that's happened in your life has led you to this point. Some of it has been great but, as is often the case, the easy stuff doesn't teach us as many lessons as the tough times. *Bob*, ever the protective parent, is always on the lookout for things that might harm you. He focuses more attention on the things that have hurt you than the things that have been achieved easily. Rather than continuing to hang on to all that negativity, wouldn't it be nicer to recognise that it's served a purpose, thank it and then respectfully let it go without regret, spite or remorse?

Tidy by category, not location: KonMari identifies five categories to work through when tidying up, as listed below. While relevant to tidying your household, I've applied them to our goal of reinventing ourselves. The reinvention categories listed are part of who we are, so we will probably bring them into most of the situations we find ourselves in throughout our lives. Remember, *Bob* will be cringing as you start to focus on the things that have up to now made you the person you are and he will try to distract you from getting to the bottom of the pile. If you jump from one category to another without really tidying it up, then you're playing into his hands.

STAGE 2: REALITY CHECK

KONMARI CATEGORIES	REINVENTION INTERPRETATION	REINVENTION CATEGORIES
Clothes	What we wear is our personal uniform. Our clothes signify how we see ourselves and how we fit into our world, including which tribe we belong to, and can reflect our self-esteem. Our titles are another type of clothing. They can be formal or informal, such as CEO, mum, retiree, divorcee, boring, focused.	Titles
Books	Books represent the knowledge, skills and interests we have collected across our lives.	Capabilities
Papers	Those everyday tasks that can distract us from our real goal and finding the joy we desire. By only hanging on to stuff that helps us and organising and filing the rest, we make space to get on with it.	Tasks
Komono (aka Miscellaneous Items)	Often, we collect many habits that serve to help us avoid facing our real issues. Computer games and mobile phones are great at distracting us from being present.	Distractions
Sentimental Items	Think of your values, beliefs, personality, mindset and self-perception and ego. This category also relates to those friends and family members who no longer fit with our lives.	Inner you

Follow the right order: The categories are arranged so that the more superficial things are dealt with first. This helps *Bob* become accustomed to the process of tidying. Things like titles are nice, but they can be taken away and may change over time. While we love that people pay us compliments and show respect to us based on the titles we wear, the importance we place on them can mask the deeper issues we have been able to hide ... until now. I can tell you after watching my mum deal with cancer that someone fighting for their life doesn't care too much if they're a general manager or CEO or not. Like COVID-19, cancer and many other life-changing catalysts help us see what is truly important.

Ask yourself if it sparks joy: OK, I have to admit, I love this. How great would our lives be if we were to measure every aspect by how much joy it sparks? Joy is an amazing feeling and if we could minimise those aspects of our lives that don't bring us joy it would lead to a happier state of mind and a more content life.

Hopefully by now you should have a really clear picture of the person you are and how you have come to find yourself in this current situation. You should be ready to move into the next step of reinvention with a more streamlined you, unburdened by the things that may have been holding you back or sabotaging your past efforts. You may feel a little raw after facing some of the realities that *Bob* has successfully kept hidden from you for too long. But don't worry, because self-evaluation is a necessary phase you need to go through before you can begin to empower yourself.

STAGE 2: REALITY CHECK

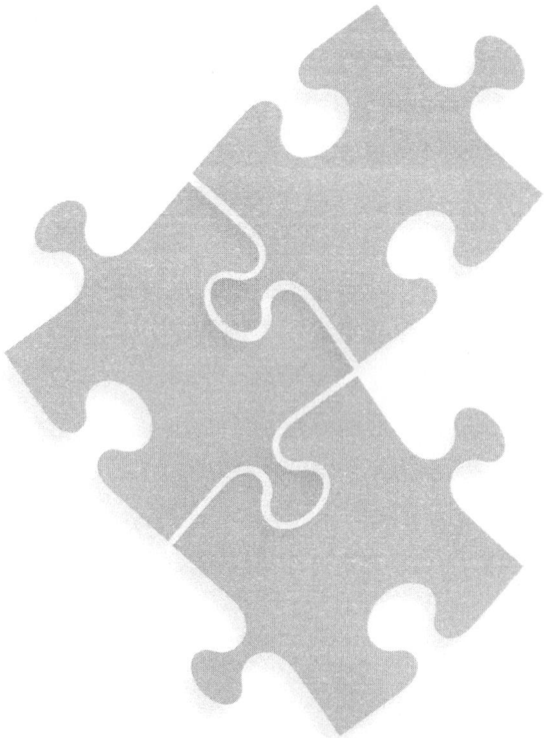

Stage 3: Empower Yourself

"Learn the rules like a pro, so you can break them like an artist".

— Pablo Picasso

STAGE 3: EMPOWER YOURSELF

Let's bounce

Any life-changing event that was the catalyst that forced you to abandon your normal, and previous identity, will eventually be followed by events that will again challenge your new existence. The first catalyst broke the patterns of your previous existence and sent you careening towards a new normal. The factors outlined in "Holy crap!" will determine how long you spend in the various stages of the grief cycle. Regardless of how long you lick your wounds, *Bob*, as a creature of habit, will quickly adapt to this new state of being and start trying to convince you to stay here, because it's better than the unknown. To break out of your new less-than-ideal state, there needs to be a second intervention or catalyst; whether internal or external, some force is required to break your uncomfortable equilibrium.

Think of these forces as being like a bungy cord. I am a big guy at 105 kg (trust me, all muscle! No, really, it is … oh, whatever) so when I jump from the safety of the platform I will descend faster and further than someone who is 50 kg. If the bungy jump is over a river, my ass is getting wet. The bungy cord stretches to a point where it starts to rebound. In this analogy, the weight is equivalent to the importance you placed on your previous life. The more it means to you, the more weight it has and the further you're likely to fall – and the further you have to travel to come back up. Even after the bounce stops at the top, you don't end up exactly where you started – you still need to be let down to the recovery point.

Bungy jumping is the battle of two forces: gravity, which is what causes the fall, and the bungy cord's elasticity and strength, which determines how quickly you rebound. Without the second catalyst of the bungy cord you would stay stuck at the bottom of the fall, which is not only uncomfortable, but could leave you feeling lost and abandoned.

One of my startups that launched with a great amount of fanfare and media attention was called localyokl. We thought it was the perfect business in that it was focused on connecting travellers with locals so that they could enjoy an authentic local experience. The concept was about personalised experiences that avoided the group tour pitfalls and let people enjoy a place exactly how they wanted with locals who shared common interests. The media loved the concept, government tourism associations were supporting us, and we also benefited from large government grants. It was an exciting time – we were being lauded as the type of digital business that could grow to be a global success.

Guides were signing up in droves because they were able to get paid to do what they loved and share their passion with interesting people from around the world. For me personally it felt like everything was finally coming together, combining the things I loved: business, innovation, travel and marketing. We knew it was going to be a slog and I started chasing investors from day one because I knew the idea was a winner. However, after four months of launching, we still weren't getting the sales we needed and the money was running on fumes. We even spent our last dollars with some digital marketing specialists to help us discover the secret sauce recipe that would bring the customers in, but they also failed to deliver. After another few months trying to survive and attract investors, we had nothing left in the tank. Broken promises from our "specialists" killed the last of our enthusiasm and drained the bank balance. After 16 months, the dream was put on ice and it was time to regroup.

I wore the failure heavily and it dragged me down to a dark place. Even in my dark place, which was very deep, I knew I had to keep doing whatever I needed to do to survive. Survival is not necessarily about moving forward or recovery; it can be just not sinking any further. Metaphorically, I was hovering just above the river on my bungy cord. Interestingly, while this all played out prior to AI becoming mainstream, much of what we offered can now be achieved with a simple prompt, excluding of course the human connections.

Fortunately, my experience with reinvention means I can easily adapt to finding a new role. But I didn't rebound straight away. Despite my good fortune of quickly finding a well-paying gig, I was unable to let go of the feeling that I was a complete failure and the urge to hide away.

When my wife saw that I was wallowing longer than could be considered healthy she said something profound, which was the external force that started me on the way back up. Her intervention boiled down to this: "You need to do something to get out of the dark place you're hiding in. This is not good for you and it's not fair to me – or us."

That was the kick in the ass I needed to get out of my own head and start seeking some help. Whether it was her infinite wisdom (she will definitely say it was this) or good timing, she knew that even if I didn't care about myself too much at that time, I wouldn't want to take anyone else down with me. With that one chat she helped me to look forward again, instead of hovering over the water while I relived the failures of my past.

While I needed to progress through my stages of grief, I knew I still needed to function – however, before that chat with my wife, my care factor was pretty close to zero. At some stage in our lives, we have all existed in a kind of purgatory where we go about our daily tasks with a level of disinterest that can feel zombie-like. It feels unreal, unfair and often never-ending, regardless of the event that sent you into the land of the living dead. Some of us will live the rest of our mortal lives locked away by the stories *Bob* tells us. But hopefully, there will be something that breaks or disrupts the pattern he has us imprisoned in. You need a reason to escape the new normal *Bob* has created for you.

Back to our bungy jump. Until the force to bounce back is greater than the force to keep falling, you will continue to descend. Eventually the forces will be equal and at that point you will become stationary, neither falling nor ascending. You end up just hanging there, looking around, waiting for the next forces to impact you.

In the world of bungy jumping we have guides to help us and keep us safe, and recovery people ready to save us should we fall. However, in the real world, we don't always have those people there to protect us and ensure we recover. At least, you may not recognise them at first. The guides you encounter in your day-to-day life can be those who care about you, such as friends, family or work colleagues; they could be frustrated associates, like the boss who fired you or the manager who needs you to change; or they could be you personally. If you were writing a movie script or book, these guides would be called archetypes and you, as the main character, would be referred to as the protagonist in your own life story.

Writing your life story

Lights, camera, action!

Who hasn't imagined writing a film script or a book? As someone who has done both I can tell you that whenever I share with someone that I've written a story they inevitably start outlining a plot or story *they* believe would be the next blockbuster or bestseller. The saying goes that everyone has at least one book in them, so here's your chance to plan the plot of yours.

First, let's start with a pop quiz: what do *Jaws*, *Love Actually*, *Dumb and Dumber* and *The Shawshank Redemption* all have in common? If you answered, "They're all movies", you get one point. If you answered, "They must be Gary's favourite movies", you lose three points (*Jaws* scared the crap out of me! I still hear the music in my head when I swim and it's been more than 40 years since I saw it). If you said "The plots are all very similar", then you win the bonus prize and the kewpie doll.

Make up your own mind based on my pitch below for this good-natured comedy of misadventure that brings together the heart of *Forgetting Sarah Marshall* and *The Secret Life of Walter Mitty* with the craziness of *Dumb and Dumber*.

> *What does a naïve, big-hearted tech billionaire do when his Russian Victoria's Secret model girlfriend steals his fortune, leaving him penniless, homeless and lost? He embarks on a journey of self-discovery that takes him from San Francisco to Hawaii, Australia and Bali. With the help of hardened surfer legend Bunga, he becomes a big-wave surfer and of course, wins the girl.*

Sounds exactly like *Jaws*, right? OK, maybe not the storyline, but dig deeper and you'll see that the story progresses through very similar stages. In fact, nearly every movie you've ever seen follows a similar arc. It's called the Hero's Journey and it can apply to your life story too. Regardless of whether you see yourself as a hero or not, you're the main character in your journey through life.

The Hero's Journey is a structural plot format thats been around for centuries. The format includes a hero (you), quests (what you desire), tests (the challenges you face), rewards (the wins you have along the way) and mentors (those who help guide you on your journey). Below is an outline of the format and how it applies to our lives.

Let's use *Love Actually* as an example, because most people would have seen it at least once, if not twenty-odd times if they watch it every Christmas. The story starts out in the hero's **Ordinary World.**

The movie introduces the characters and their everyday lives, and each character has some endearing traits that help us connect to them and leave us wanting to know more. In *Love Actually* this was the airport scene, which set the mood and tone of the film. It's also where we returned at the end when all the storylines were wrapped up. If your personal catalyst was a relationship breakdown then the camera would capture you doing something you loved together; if it was a job redundancy, then the opening image would see you winning at work. These are the scenes that *Bob* will play in your head when things start to get tough. There may also be some hints that things are not as ideal as they seem.

Once we become familiar with the normal life and the characters there will be a **Call to Adventure**. This is an incident that draws our hero in and becomes the catalyst for the changes they will experience. This is where we learn what's wrong with the story we've been sold as cracks start to appear. Think: Billy *Bob* Thornton as the US president asserting his dominance over Hugh Grant as Britain's prime minister, or Emma Thompson and Alan Rickman's portrayal of a comfortable but slightly stale relationship. Then, *boom!* the **Catalyst** appears and challenges the protagonist's view of their world. It looks like Billy *Bob* Thornton making a move on Hugh Grant's love interest or Alan Rickman buying the necklace for his assistant. In the real world this could be discovering your partner is cheating on you, losing your job, winning the lottery or any other life-changing event.

The next stage is the **Refusal of the Call** and this is when the hero tries to avoid the inevitable. *Bob* will use the fear of the unknown to try to stop you making further changes as you debate the

STAGE 3: EMPOWER YOURSELF

consequences of doing nothing or stepping up and facing the challenge. This is when *Bob* really puts on a performance, going over your weaknesses and fears on repeat and turning up the volume to the max. In *Love Actually* Hugh Grant transfers his love interest to another role, while Emma Thompson's character pretends she doesn't know about the necklace. In the real world this might look like trying to patch things up with your cheating ex, refusing to apply for new jobs, or pretending you didn't win big in Powerball. You can't hide forever, though; eventually you'll have to make a choice about what to do based on the options available to you. This is decision time, and your options range from staying where you are, going backward or moving forward.

All the previous chapters of this book form Act One of your movie. When you've decided to answer the call, you move into Act Two, where you will need guidance and support to face the unknown. Acts Two and Three make up the remainder of this book.

Before you can continue with your story you need to do something that you may have been avoiding – make a **Choice**. Sometimes the options available to us won't be particularly appealing. When my mum was diagnosed with cancerous sarcoma in her lower leg, the options available to her were amputation or accept that the cancer would spread throughout her body and she would die pretty quickly. Neither option was rainbows and lollipops but she had a choice to make, and even avoiding it was choosing certain death in a short timeframe. To make this incredibly tough decision, Mum went looking for the people who could help, including doctors, support people, family and friends, and cancer survivors. Armed with their information Mum made her choice, had her leg amputated, and in script-writing terms crossed the threshold. **Crossing the Threshold** does not guarantee an easy journey but it forces you out of wallowing and provides a way forward.

Being risk-averse, *Bob* will begin frantically looking through his files of our past experiences to find those that can be applied in our current situation. In the absence of similar experiences, he will start exploring externally for information that can inform the decision and provide greater certainty of a successful outcome. In film, this will be when the hero meets people who help and guide him on his journey. In the movie *Shrek*, Donkey and Princess are mentors who help Shrek answer the call and start the adventure to his new normal. In your case, it could be a family member or friend who provides advice in a supportive way, or it might be a mentor, such as a disgruntled boss or loved one, who shoves you towards answering the call of your personal journey.

Along your journey you will inevitably experience more tests. You'll be helped by allies and hindered by antagonists who will divert you from your quest if you don't recognise them and disarm their influence over you. In *Shrek*, Lord Farquaad is the antagonist, Donkey is an ally and the tests are both internal (Shrek's self-doubt) and external (presented by Lord Farquaad). If you're going through a relationship break-up, the antagonist will be played by your ex and the allies are your family, friends and professional counsellors or therapists. The tests will be many as you and your ex navigate your way through the pain and problems that brought you to this point.

Of course, a story wouldn't be realistic if it didn't come with the twists and turns that challenge us and force us to grow as we search for the reward of a new and hopefully better life. For Mum, the weekend before her surgery was very traumatic and sad. She was saying goodbye to her leg and in her mind, her identity as an abled person. The grief was heart-wrenching. She would dance around the lounge room in tears, filled with the despair that she would never dance on two legs again. We all shed tears as she **Approached the Ordeal** of losing her leg. If your wife left you, then the approach to your ordeal could be going to see a divorce lawyer and the ordeal would be the divorce itself, or it could be coming to terms with the idea that you are good enough to be loved. If you have found yourself unemployed, then the approach could be cleaning out your desk and the ordeal would be coming to terms with being unemployed and beginning the process of finding a new job.

In *Shrek*, the **Reward** was the love of Princess Fiona. Even though it wasn't why Shrek started the journey, it became the holy grail of rewards; it was all he could focus on once it revealed itself. The journey on the **Road Back** will not necessarily be smooth either, because we're navigating paths that we have never had to travel before. There will be false starts, steps backward and disappointments, but these tests help us find our way and adapt to our new normal. Job rejections, bad first dates, self-doubt, reactions to chemo – these are all challenges we may face along the journey.

Then when it comes together and you've landed the new job, or you've made peace with being single, or finished chemo and got the all clear, your acceptance of your new normal is the equivalent of the triumphant hero **Returning With the Elixir or Reward**. You're ready to move forward and thrive in this world.

Cut, check the gate, that's a wrap. And just like that, your life story has been captured forever until the next great adventure.

STAGE 3: EMPOWER YOURSELF

Which way?

Sidekicks and mentors are often underappreciated in movies. Donkey in *Shrek*, the gal squad in *Sex in the City*, Odin in *Thor* – the list goes on. The role they play is to not only provide a sounding board but challenge the protagonist's beliefs that are holding them back. Think about your favourite movie and you will no doubt identify allies, real or perceived, who helped the main character through their journey. In *Shrek*, Donkey appeared to be an annoying sidekick. He was funny AF, yes, but how much he helped Shrek on his journey seemed questionable. But if you rewatch it to see if there's more to Donkey than his wit and humour, you'll see that Donkey's antics and faults actually helped Shrek challenge his misperceptions, face his fears and move forward to a better place with Princess Fiona by his side.

As the star of our own story we often need help and guidance when we find ourselves stuck in uncomfortable or unhealthy territory or trekking down unfamiliar paths with lots of twists and turns. How heavily we are impacted and our response to the challenges and fears we may experience as a result will determine how long our bounce takes after we hit rock bottom. Having made the choice to brush ourselves off and get up again to embark on the next stage of our journey, and having figured out what we want to take with us and what we need to leave behind, we look for a way forward. In *Alice in Wonderland,* Lewis Carroll makes this insightful observation:

> One day Alice came to a fork in the road and saw a Cheshire cat in a tree. "Which road do I take?" she asked. "Where do you want to go?" was his response. "I don't know," Alice answered. "Then," said the cat, "it doesn't matter."

One of the first steps in making a choice about where we want to go is to explore options. Sometimes the options are very limited, like when Mum was presented with the choice of amputate or die, while at other times we have too many options, and we can become stuck in analysis paralysis, where we never feel appropriately armed with enough information to make a decision with 100% confidence. This is me when deciding which new car I should buy. I frustrate my wife no end with my procrastination. *Bob* works me over with thoughts like: *What if a new model is coming soon? Is there something I might like even more? Should I spend less money or more money?* Which could explain why my Jeep now has more than 400,000 kilometres on the clock. As my wife says to me in a frustrated, but *loving* tone: "Just make a fucking decision, any decision!" (I must admit, it's getting hard to distinguish the loving tone, as frustration accompanied by a 360-degree eyeroll seems to be her dominant emotion, but I keep telling myself it's underpinned with love.)

STAGE 3: EMPOWER YOURSELF

If I'm stuck, I check in with *Bob* to see why he's making this such a big thing and what fears might be holding me back, as well as what additional information would help me make a choice. The fear of making the wrong decision and having buyer's remorse is one of the forces *Bob* and I regularly battle with.

One way to gather information is to log onto AI and look for similar situations and advice. While this is a great way to learn about something (and on YouTube you can even find videos of people sharing their experiences and advice), for me personally, it's like trying to learn to drive or do brain surgery by watching a video. Even armed with all my shiny new knowledge I would still have trouble actually driving a car, and I reluctantly admit that coming to me for neurosurgery would not be a great idea despite me being a qualified senior first aid instructor.

Another approach is to find people who have been where you are and succeeded, coming through even stronger as a result of what they have endured. Imagine trying to qualify for the Olympics. This is a huge goal and to achieve it you would need to find a coach who can guide you to your success. The role of the coach is not only to teach you the finer parts of your chosen sport but also know you to such an extent that they understand your weaknesses and strengths, and when to push you and when to support you. It's their job to help you exceed your personal limitations and continue to improve so that you are podium material. Athletes use coaches, actors use coaches and even the most successful in business engage coaches and mentors to help them achieve their goals. AI will even evolve to enable us to access 'virtual' coaches who are completely dedicated to us and our goals, available at any hour of the day and at no cost.

Usually there is an endless range of mentors who will magically appear when you have made your choice and start sharing your goals. Some will be professional, some will be close friends and family, some will be strangers, and some will mean well, while others will take perverse pleasure in seeing you stay stuck. The trick is being able to recognise the mentors you should listen to and those you should avoid.

The types of mentors you may encounter include:

Besties: These are the close friends in your life who are well meaning and want the best for you. They can be protective and, like *Bob*, want you to avoid further pain, which means they can sometimes be too supportive when you need someone to give you a push. They are great supports as we are coming to terms with our grief, but the question is: can they change tack to help us grow when we're ready? At times like this we need people who push us forward and challenge us rather than encourage us to stay stagnant or, even worse, return to the world that caused the pain, such as a dysfunctional relationship.

Tough love: This term was made famous by Dr Phil from *Oprah*. When someone was making excuses and blaming others for not moving forward, he would tell them exactly what was holding them back, and often it was the jolt they needed to start their journey.

STAGE 3: EMPOWER YOURSELF

The Oracle: The wise one who has taken this path before and, like the character in the movie *The Matrix*, can provide guidance on how to navigate the obstacles that may arise. They may have coached or counselled others along similar journeys with success.

Role models: These people are similar to the Oracle; they are those you look up to as good examples of people who have succeeded. Sometimes our role models are famous and are known for their success in returning from challenges and hardship, while others can be found much closer to home in our support network. Mine include my parents, my wife and my ex-wife.

Emotional vampires: These are the friends or acquaintances who come looking to feed off any negativity you may be holding. They have this supernatural skill of being able to help you see the negative in any situation and return you to the dark state you're trying to emerge from. They may appear to be lovely and supportive at first but the tell-tale sign of an emotional vampire is if you feel drained and down after spending time with them. It's best to move towards the light because we know that vampires prefer the darkness of the shadows.

Anchors: These are the people who don't want you to move forward. Due to their own self-worth issues or the ongoing effects of their own challenges, they would prefer you remained stuck with them. They usually appear very understanding and share familiar stories about being stuck in the darkness. It's great to have a buddy who relates to what you're going through, but even better to have someone who can help you move forward. *Bob* will already be trying to hold you back so you don't need others joining the Negative Nelly parties.

Mentors can take many forms; they can exist in the physical realm or live within the memories you have of inspirational people. Some of your mentors will have characteristics of several of the types listed above. The lessons mentors provide us with can be positive and push us forward, or they might appear negative at first, like Donkey in *Shrek*, to help us understand why we can't stay stuck in nowhere land. Here are a couple of simple questions to guide you in entrusting your journey with the range of mentors you will meet:

- Have they experienced similar situations to the one you are navigating?

- Do you believe they have your best interests at heart?

- Are they speaking the truth, regardless of how hard it is to hear?

- Are they living a life you can connect with?

- Should you and will you listen to them?

- Are they deserving of your trust?

Before you blindly follow the advice of your cherished mentors there is one warning to always keep in mind: they are not you. This is really important, because if they tell you they know exactly what you're going through and therefore the perfect way for you to move forward, they can lead you astray. Smile, listen and then get *Bob* to filter what you have heard against your own experiences. Regardless of how well informed they are, the experiences they had or how much you respect them, they can only speak from their perspective. What works for you may be very close to what they offered, but it won't be exact – and nor should it be, as they haven't lived your life or share all your beliefs and values. You have to do what feels right for you while taking pieces of advice from your mentors to help you evolve.

One last point: keep in mind that advice and opinions are like buttholes – most people have one, so be careful you aren't taking their shit on board.

Facing fears, (fears blame and loathing)

Mentors are fantastic to help guide us through our journey and talk through the fears we may develop along the way. However, fears are as unique as we are, and despite the best intentions of family, friends and others, only you can face your fears. Sometimes we look to people to protect us from our fears, but this doesn't always work given that the origins of our fears can stem from a range of past personal experiences or our perception of those experiences. For instance, a fear of heights could come from overprotective parents who warned you when you were young not to climb that tree because you could fall and hurt yourself. Others may be the result of something that triggered an emotional event that scarred you.

I grew up in New Guinea and lived an idyllic childhood playing with the locals and swimming out on the reefs. Dad tells me stories of going fishing and seeing sharks so huge that they would extend

STAGE 3: EMPOWER YOURSELF

far beyond the front and back of our large boat. Sharks were just part of life and while they were something to be wary of, they didn't play much of a part in what I got up to. Then in 1975, the movie *Jaws* was released. Mum and Dad tried to make sure my sister and I didn't see it, but as a stubborn and sneaky 12-year-old, I managed to defy them, and holy crap! It was life-changing.

From that point onwards I was petrified of any body of water. The joy I found in swimming in oceans was torn away and my irrational fear extended to fresh-water dams and swimming pools at night. I even considered the possibility of sharks swimming up through the drains into my path. Watching *Jaws* became a major life-changing event that stayed with me for about 30 years and tore away my love of the water. My mentors, such as Mum and Dad, would try to explain to me that I was being silly and tried to help me come to my senses by being supportive or showing tough love in equal amounts. Nothing worked because they couldn't see the story *Bob* had created for me. Diving into water triggered *Bob* to play the iconic soundtrack and shock me with mental images of a shark coming out of the water with its teeth bared, ready to attack. I would be lucky if I could last more than a couple of minutes before I would need to jump out, feeling equal amounts of shame, disappointment, foolishness and relief for being back on dry land. I was no longer able to enjoy one of my greatest pleasures. Screw you, *Bob*!

That's the thing with *Bob*: he can BS with the best of them and spin a great story to get his way. While our fears can be valid, like standing on a cliff and being scared of falling, often the fears that are holding us back are built on one basic fear – and that is the fear of failure. Being afraid of getting hurt in a relationship, not getting another job, never achieving success again, trying to learn to walk or talk again after a stroke and not being able to, fighting cancer and losing the battle, or public speaking or learning a new skill – they all boil down to a fear of failure.

Fear of failure can disguise itself in many forms and *Bob* is great at finding the form that will be most effective in stopping us changing and exposing ourselves to emotional pain. Procrastination, apathy, distractions, negative self-talk, prolonged self-pity and analysis paralysis are all symptoms of *Bob* working you over with the fear of failure. Whenever I sit down to write *Bob* comes in with some not-so-helpful thoughts. Entering my office with an enthusiastic commitment to knocking out a couple of chapters, I can be quickly put off as *Bob* starts to question if I can do this, whether the thoughts will flow, and if the words make sense.

As the words get louder in my head *Bob* gets sneaky and starts presenting reasons not to put my thinking cap on. Behind the fridge needs cleaning; I need to organise my library not only alphabetically, but by colour, topic and size; and I wonder what a 1964 Kombi is currently selling for. Then I'll remember that I haven't chatted to my second cousin removed on my mother's side ever, so I should really give them a call. Any excuse will do for *Bob* to keep me from exposing myself to failure. The annoying thing is that all too often he gets his way and I'm left wondering where the day went after spending eight hours googling new mullet hairstyles.

Other names I considered for this chapter were "F#ck fear" or "Become fearless" but I realised they were not realistic. After all, our fears are very real in our own minds. They may be irrational, baseless and seriously annoying, but to us, they are as real as the ground our feet stand on. Trying to say we can just turn them on and off at our whim diminishes their impact and sets us up for failure, which is often what we're trying to avoid in the first place. Equally, to think that we will ever be completely fearless also fails the reality test. We need our fears and they serve a purpose to ensure we properly consider the consequences of our actions.

In his book *Outliers*, Malcom Gladwell writes that it takes 10,000 hours to master anything. It seems like a lot of hours, but if you consider how much time *Bob* spends obsessing and thinking about your fears, you realise how much they are a part of your everyday. Sadly, rather than us beating our fears, it's more likely that our fears have used that time to master us.

Often, doing the very thing we are most scared of is the only true way to challenge the stories and images *Bob* has created. My fear of sharks diminished over time thanks to a couple of actions I took to face it. It started when I went diving in Thailand with harmless leopard sharks and started to realise that Bruce, the shark from *Finding Nemo*, wasn't sitting under the surface, waiting to munch on me as soon as I jumped in the water. The second reality check came when my wife and I went diving with grey nurse sharks at an aquarium where the huge sharks would swim right at you until you ducked under them. Apparently, they like the feeling of bubbles on their tummies ... cute, right? From these small initial steps I have now reached the point where I am an avid surfer and have reclaimed my joy of being in the water. It's worth noting that I still get flashes of my debilitating fear, but my experiences in facing it have enabled me to keep moving forward so I'm not left sitting on the shore, missing out on my life.

Some of the symptoms of *Bob* using your fears to control you include:

Avoidance: You may be avoiding facing the reality of the situation, making a decision, or taking action. Avoidance can be either a conscious response or a subconscious reaction, where *Bob* creates a scenario that distracts you or enables you to avoid dealing with reality. I gave up water sports as a result of my fear of Jaws. *Bob* argued that water sports weren't that important to me and he would bombard my mind with images of gnashing shark teeth with a severe overbite.

Procrastination: The close cousin of avoidance is procrastination. *Bob* uses procrastination as a powerful tool that allows you to seem like you are focused on getting on with it, while distracting you from actually doing anything. The list of distractions *Bob* is able to conjure up is endless, fascinating, and when you think about them, often hilarious. "Research" is another excuse *Bob* may present to help you justify procrastinating and getting nothing done.

Anxiety: Feeling stressed, on edge, touchy or distracted are all signs of anxiety. When *Bob* feels threatened by something that he knows you are afraid of, he will invoke the fight, flight or freeze response sequences discussed earlier. Regardless of which one he chooses you will find yourself experiencing some short-term changes in response to your fears. The physical impacts mean that your body has increased your heart rate; adrenaline floods your tissues, getting your muscles ready to flee; and you may experience tunnel focus as you assess and manage your fears. The longer fear affects you, the more long-term impacts of anxiety you will experience. High blood pressure, decreased immunity, exhaustion and greater vulnerability to external factors are medically recognised impacts of being stressed for too long.

Irritability: Due to *Bob* demanding your full attention on your fears you will have reduced capacity to deal with distractions that are not directly associated with whatever fear you are dealing with. This is no time for niceties, *Bob* would argue, due to your super-focused state. Think of what happens when you try talking to someone engrossed in a video game.

Depression: If the impact of your fears on the things that are important to you drags on, then your anxious state could tread into the dark forest of depression. Hope and action are elements that shine light on the path out of the darkness.

Blaming: One of the ways *Bob* likes to protect you is to ensure you appear blameless when you're avoiding your fears. By diverting blame onto someone else, *Bob* reasons you will be less inclined to feel like you need to change. This redirection of responsibility is a powerful tool. Research has shown that we are more likely to judge others harshly for doing something unethical than if we did the same thing ourselves. *Bob* will find many justifications for our actions. For example, when someone cuts me off in traffic I get cranky and mild road rage ensues. However, if I cut someone off, my *Bob* quickly works to convince me that they must have been speeding and that was why I didn't see them, that someone must have moved my mirrors, or that they should have realised I needed to change lanes for the upcoming exit. Notice the art of diversion and manipulation that *Bob* is a master of: everyone else is at fault other than me, of course. If I buy into this, then I will be less inclined to change and face the fears associated with failure and the unknown. However, despite *Bob*'s mastery, we often start to get a feeling of dissatisfaction that can grow into self-loathing as we recognise that we're not taking control of our life and making the changes we need to make. Regardless of who is to blame, we are the only ones who can take control of making changes.

If I had to choose one fear out of all of them to focus on, it would have to be the fear of failure. It is by far our biggest and most debilitating fear and it can be dressed up in many guises as fear of change, fear of public speaking, fear of relationships – fear of most things. Except of course, sharks – those things are real and have big scary teeth.

STAGE 3: EMPOWER YOURSELF

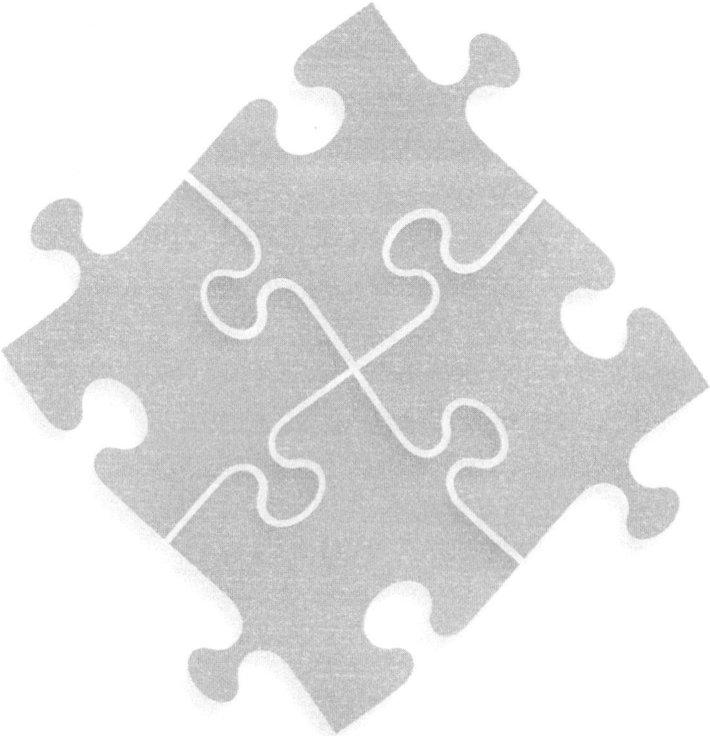

Stage 4: Action

"Even if you are on the right track, you'll get run over if you just sit there".

— Will Rogers

STAGE 4: ACTION

Do something, anything

As a kid, I was afraid of the dark. In my mind there were monsters lurking in the dark, ready to jump out and grab me whenever I let my guard down. It was very similar to my irrational fear of sharks. As an adult, I no longer think there are monsters hiding in every dark spot, but I'm still more of a Disney guy than a Stephen King scary movie fan. I really don't get why people enjoy being scared, and when I do reluctantly watch horror movies (through my fingers so I can block out the scary parts, of course) I never understand why people venture into the attic or basement when everybody knows that's where evil awaits. But unlike the unsuspecting babysitter in the horror movies, when we find ourselves in life-changing situations, we always have a choice. We can either face our fears or we can close the door to the attic and let our fears debilitate us, define us and hold us back.

THE POWER OF STARTING

To start a journey from your current state of normal requires you to do things differently, as this will directly or indirectly result in change. Sometimes, doing nothing may seem like the safe option, but over time the monsters may find you, or life and opportunities may pass you by. A lump in your breast may be curable, but the longer you ignore it, the greater the chance that your fate will be decided for you. A career break could be great for revitalising or refocusing, but the longer it goes on, the more outdated your skills may become or the greater your self-doubt will be. Inaction without a plan or reason can lead to your situation deteriorating and often increases the possibility of negative outcomes. Monsters left unconfronted can leave us stuck in middle of nowhere, cowering instead of living our best life. If you can't think of where to start you could always detail your dilemma into AI and ask it to provide a plan to move forward. Even just seeing an outline in writing will help solidify which plan is best for you.

The factors that determine whether we start our journey to venture beyond our current state of normality are our level of dissatisfaction, our degree of confidence, our vision for our future and the plan we have to achieve it.

THE NEGATIVES OF LUCK

Beware, though: often, *Bob* will use visions of luck and fate as part of his justification to stay stuck as you wait for good fortune to smile on you. He may pepper your thoughts with comments like "the universe will provide" or "if it's meant to be then it will happen" as part of his reasoning for not taking action. Don't act, he whispers, wait and see how it unfolds. This is the equivalent of using the lottery as your investment strategy for your future. Sure, it happens for some of us, but unless you're the one in a million that the gods smile on then maybe hedging your bets by actually doing something to improve your situation could add to your chances of success.

THE POSITIVES OF DISSATISFACTION

One of the CEOs I once worked with had a management philosophy that took me some time to fully appreciate. Rob looked for and even demanded a level of dissatisfaction in his people. Now, admit it: when you read this your first reaction was WTF! What sort of dictator or psychopathic boss looks to actively encourage and support his staff being dissatisfied? On the surface it goes against almost every management theory and personal wellbeing philosophy out there; high levels of satisfaction and acceptance are all the rage. But Rob's logic is that if you're satisfied with where you are right now then why bother changing? What's the motivation to go through the effort and discomfort of growing and moving from your current state? Even Buddhism is based on the idea that you need to grow in this lifetime to reach the next level of enlightenment to move forward into the next.

The power of the state of dissatisfaction is in where your focus is. If your dissatisfaction encourages you to grow to a state of normality that improves your world, then it's a positive dissatisfaction. However, if your dissatisfaction gives *Bob* ammunition to stop you moving forward or sends you further into a dark place, then you may need to take further action on management strategies for *Bob* to balance out your attachment to the negative dissatisfaction.

CREATE URGENCY

The problem with planning is that sometimes *Bob* can use this as an illusion that you're actually doing something. A well-thought-out and robust plan is important but trying to cover every outcome or possibility can be time consuming and self-defeating. Eventually you have to put your big boy or girl pants on and jump in. Of course, *Bob* will freak out at this action and argue that there are many reasons why you shouldn't jump. So set a start time and create some urgency; you aren't getting any younger and you aren't moving forward either. There's a great quote I came across through group work in counselling that sums up the thought process involved in a sense of urgency. *"If not me, then who? If not now, then when? If not here, then where?"*

These simple questions take you through a series of personal reflections that address the categories of excuses *Bob* may offer up to convince you that the time is not right, or you need to be in a different place to make the change. There may be some truth in the argument that right now isn't perfect, but chances are that unless you're in a fight, flight or freeze situation, such as hanging off a cliff with one hand, it's more likely that you're suffering a case of excusitis, which can be cured by simply doing something.

BUILD CONFIDENCE

Just as kryptonite is Superman's weakness, action is the antidote for fear, procrastination and inaction. One trick to building confidence for taking action is to make sure you set achievable targets that allow you to have small wins along the way, so you know you're actually getting somewhere and don't become disillusioned. This is where most of us fall down. We have such grandiose visions but without planning the steps to get there, those visions remain dreams rather than a future reality.

Our vision is what helps us stay committed and on the path, while the small steps and wins are what keeps us motivated to complete the journey. Because we're embarking on an unfamiliar path *Bob* will be on high alert, trying to protect us from failure. The more we can prove to him that this is achievable, the more willing he will be to get on board. Think about when you learned to drive. When you started you were probably very focused on every little thing that you needed to do and what could go wrong. The more you did it, the more your confidence grew and the stronger the neural pathways became so that your new skill of driving became a habit requiring little conscious thought at all. Confidence is about *Bob* knowing you've got this, and the only way he will reach that conclusion is if you take action, repeat it until it becomes ingrained, and consistently achieve success.

Think of the forces acting on your current state of normal like standing in a body of water. Depending on what is happening in your life you may be standing in a stagnant pond, a slow stream or fast-moving rapids. If you're standing in a pond, eventually the water will become slimy and mould will start to grow. As the water starts to smell, you'll develop a greater risk of picking up some sort of infection from the festering bacteria.

However, if you're crossing a fast-moving stream, trying to force your way through will lead to you quickly tiring, losing your motivation and getting washed away. But if you move with the direction of the current, then the forces will help you get to where you want to be.

As a keen surfer I'm very conscious of rips in the surf. A rip is when large amounts of water move away from the shore in a narrow current. If you're a swimmer you don't want to get caught in a rip as it can take you out beyond the waves into the deep water. The rule is, if you get caught in a rip, don't try and swim against the current as you will quickly tire and could drown. Instead of fighting the current you should relax and go with it, and when it drops you beyond the waves you can swim back in, away from the rip. For a surfer, however, rips are like an escalator to the back of the waves. Using it saves my arms from having to paddle all that way. Depending on the circumstances rips can either help you or kill you – you just need to be aware of them and know how to utilise their power rather than fight against insurmountable currents.

- There are more surfer lessons that apply to taking action in everyday life. Some of my favourites are:

- Remain flexible – sometimes what we thought was the best way to reach our goals will change as a result of forces beyond our control.

STAGE 4: ACTION

- Sometimes the best rides are from the waves you weren't expecting.

- Don't keep fighting against the current; try to leverage the forces impacting you to find a way to keep moving towards your goal.

- Often, the way to your goals is not a straight line. Look for milestones that let you know you're still heading in the right direction.

- Keep paddling, because you never know when a break will come your way.

- Stay focused on your goal so you don't lose your way.

Think big, start small

Bill Gates once noted *"most people overestimate what they can do in one year and underestimate what they can do in ten years"*.

After paddling out through the breakers I sit on my board in the ocean, watching for the perfect wave. As I wait, I chat with my surfing buddies, 11-time world champion and GOAT (that's greatest of all time) Kelly Slater and actor Chris Hemsworth, joking about who will get the wave of the day. Then we spot it. It's a monster wall of water and it's building up to be a perfect left-hander. We all drop down onto our boards and start to paddle. Thor, despite being the god of thunder, falls away, so it's just me and Kelly. We both launch onto the wave and as we enter the barrel Kelly is knocked off. Now it's just me, and man, do I nail it! I really carve the wave up, doing some pretty rad tricks. Triumphant, I hit the beach and start walking – rather, strutting – towards Kelly and Chris when out of nowhere I feel a big shove in the back. Indignant, I turn around, and although it takes me a second to focus, I finally see my wife angrily telling me I'm snoring again. Another wet dream spoiled!

STAGE 4: ACTION

DREAM ON

Often, our new world or new normal initially manifests itself in our dreams. Dreams are a great way for our inner desires to share the picture of what our alternate life could be. The other great thing about dreams is that *Bob* naps when we nap. Almost anything can be explored in that magical world, as *Bob*'s voice of reason and negativity is silenced and we're free to discover. Even nightmares serve a purpose, as they're our subconscious unpacking the shit that may be holding us back or that keeps playing on our mind. Both types of dreams serve a purpose by letting us know that something in our world is not what we desire.

If the person in my dreams was the person I am when I'm awake I could really conquer the world. No wave would scare me, no presentation would create anxiety. I would be able to do anything I desire. It doesn't matter whether your dreams happen in your sleep or when you're daydreaming. What does matter is how motivated or attached you become to the story that your subconscious is creating for you.

WRITE DOWN YOUR GOALS

If you can't imagine yourself achieving your new normal, living the life you want or becoming the person you desire, then how can you plan what you need to do to get there? *Bob* loves fluffy ambiguity when you're planning on making a change because without a clear vision he knows he'll be able to easily distract you and convince you not to travel too far from where you are now. A great vision is one where you can describe in minute detail how you fit into it and how you will feel when you are there.

When you're visualising it's a good time to tell *Bob* to STFU, especially if he's trying to put a lid on your creativity and dreams. Be bold when you dream; you deserve it. Aim for the stars, or as Jim Collins, author of the landmark book *Good to Great*, calls them, Big, Hairy, Audacious Goals or BHAG. A BHAG is a goal that feels like it's 70% achievable, clear and compelling, pushes your boundaries and builds on your current skills, and can be measured.

The reality check you did previously now comes into play as you need to work on yourself as much as you need to work on your situation. The visualisation needs to go deep, right into the traits and values you see for yourself, without being delusional. If your mind can't show you your vision in images then a vision board is a great tool to try. Think scrapbooking with purpose as you build the story board of your new normal. The problem with vision boards is that often they are about *things*, which look great in a picture but don't provide the contentment we desire. So as you put your kindergarten scissor skills to good use, look for images that also portray the feelings and state of mind you're striving for.

ONE STEP TAKEN IS A STEP CLOSER

Once you have the big picture clear in your head you need to think about the steps involved in reaching it. The difficulty with big picture ideas is that they can seem so damn big that they feel beyond reach. When I was trekking through the Everest region

STAGE 4: ACTION

towards Gokyo Ri at 5357 metres (around the same height as Everest Base Camp), I was suffering altitude sickness, gasping for air and fighting a killer headache. Every step was a challenge that seemed to take every ounce of my physical and mental strength to keep going. In the distance was the end goal: the Gokyo Ri (peak) and our lodgings. To keep going I focused on the end goal while setting myself small achievable goals, such as taking a break after ten more steps. This allowed me to use the satisfaction of small wins to help me stay on the path to the ultimate end goal of summitting.

If you're anything like me, with the attention span of a gnat, looking too far ahead allows *Bob* too much room to introduce self-doubt or distractions to try to stop you reaching your goals. Planning small wins along the way helps him feel the satisfaction of achieving something, which releases some of the feel-good hormone dopamine, which in turn reinforces the drive for you to keep going. Every small win encourages further action and before you know it, your life has changed towards your vision.

One other trap for young players is that when we set goals, we set too many of them. We get all inspired and go for gold, figuring the more, the better. While this may be true for things such as chocolate and gold (in that order), this isn't necessarily the best way to approach goal setting. Rather, the more goals you have, the more likely you are to become overwhelmed and quit. If you want to write down 100 or 1000 goals, go for it. Get all those gems onto paper, because this lengthy list will become the framework for you to decide which is most important. Before you rate the goals in order of importance, look for those that are similar and can be grouped together. Often, goals or thoughts can be grouped under one category as they are really just different sides of the same thing. For example, if your goals are to earn more money, make your work more interesting, and have more work-from-home time, then maybe your overarching goal is to find a new job that delivers those perks.

Your dreams allow you to explore possibilities, your vision lets you visualise yourself living that life, your goals help you get where you want to go, and your plans outline the steps you need to take to get there. Tapping into your vision and goals for the journey and referring to your desired itinerary (where you plan to be and when) will help you stay on track and see how far you have come. Nelson Mandela wisely commented "It always seems impossible until it's done".

STAGE 4: ACTION

Road trip!

OK, I'll admit it: I'm a sucker for a road trip. The chance to explore, see new things, eat sugary snacks and bad service station food, and of course have a captive audience to test out my latest dad jokes and bad taste in music – what's not to love?

The secret to a successful road trip is all in the preparation: ensuring that you've considered what you might need along the way and what could go wrong. What you need to pack and prepare for depends on where you're going and how far you're travelling. A long journey means a longer classic 80s playlist and more sweets than necessary for one person – I mean, a carload of people. Get the car serviced, fill the tank, buy snacks, book motels if it's an overnighter. By doing these things you are preparing yourself for a smooth journey. Sure, things may go wrong, but hopefully you will have covered most of the contingencies.

The same is true for any journey we take. How smoothly it goes is dependent on how well planned and prepared we are. The key elements that will define its success are our knowledge of the destination and the steps involved in getting there; if we have the skills required to get there; and of course, if we have any experience we can call on along the way.

Because we are heading into downtown reinvention, a place we haven't been before, the best results and smoothest journey will be achieved through doing our research and getting ready for the trip. Sure, we could wing it and see how we go, but this laidback approach, while a lot easier initially, could lead to pain and detours along the way. Also keep in mind that *Bob* is totally uncomfortable with this change journey and will be sitting in the backseat of your mind, criticising the route and using any challenges you encounter to try to convince you to turn around and head back to your old normal.

Regardless of whether your desired destination is a new job or a better life or a cancer-free body, it's time to research and figure out what you will need in this new land. Start by chatting to your mentors or others who have made a similar journey to the one you're embarking on to understand how they approached it. You may have noticed that I used the word "similar" as even if it seems that they headed to the same destination, they are not you and therefore their journey and their destination will never be exactly the same as yours. Even if the job has the same title or you both end up leading the single life, the experience will be very different for each of you.

Your preparation includes getting a clear understanding of what you will need to know in the new land. It may be a certain qualification if you're looking to change jobs; it may be strategies

STAGE 4: ACTION

to stop falling back into negative patterns you're trying to break, such as using drugs or alcohol to excess; or it might be anticipating the emotions you may experience along the journey. AI gives us access to a wealth of information on any topic. As you dig into a subject you will find that some elements grab you more than others and this will direct you to what you should do. You can even use AI to check out podcasts, online courses, articles, TED Talks on the topic. Do everything you can to educate yourself about where to go and what to expect. Obviously, you may need to get an official bit of paper to accompany your knowledge if your new normal includes a career change.

Keep in mind, though, that while learning by reading or watching others is very useful, it's not a complete education. If I had to have brain surgery I would much prefer a doctor who has done the operation before, ideally at least a million times. This is where skills and experience come into it. Reading or watching how to do something takes you maybe twenty-five per cent of the way to mastering it; the rest of the development comes from applying the knowledge. The more you read about something, the more capable you are of talking about it, but if your aim is to make real changes, you need to do it, too.

Think about when you learned to drive a car. Depending on your age, you were probably given a book of road rules and shown clips of the basics, before you terrorised your parents and driving instructors on the roads and local shopping centre parking lots. Eventually, after many stalls, jumpy starts and stressed parents, you started to drive safely. Now, driving is second nature and many of the elements of driving that used to stress you no longer give you pause for thought.

I was going to write that you have mastered the art of driving, but then I thought about the number of people who don't indicate, cut off others, drive too slow, drive too fast, or just shouldn't be on the road (bring on driverless cars). Mastery is not the same as competence; true mastery is when you have pushed yourself to the limits and experienced the full range of possibilities involved in the discipline. It's only by testing the boundaries that you truly grow to master something. Now, this isn't for everyone. When driving, most of us will never need to be able to perform a Scandinavian flick or left-foot braking (or right-foot braking if you're in a left-hand drive country), or use an opposite lock to take corners without losing momentum. These are the outlier skills associated with mastering driving, and most of us will never need them or want them.

Probably the best way to prepare for your journey, regardless of what it is, is to make a list of the things you may need and consider the following:

- How far are you travelling from your current normal?

- Is the journey expected to be tough? What could help make it easier?

- What skills and qualifications will help you achieve your goal?

STAGE 4: ACTION

- Who can you talk to for hints and tips? Who will be your "phone a friend" person along the way to help you stay on track?

- What will you use when you get tired to keep going and avoid giving up?

- What is your stretch goal and what is the minimum you will be satisfied in achieving?

Coffee, Coke and other habits

Coffee is one of the addictions many of us share. We use it as a kick-starter in the morning, a pick-me-up throughout the day, and don't forget the most commonly used phrase for catching up: "let's do coffee". It's a stimulant, a social connector, and depending on your level of connoisseur, a passion. My personal preference is a combination of two of my addictions to create the perfect brew, which is a mocha. Chocolate and coffee: a match made in heaven.

Prior to this new love of mochas, I was addicted to Coke, as in Coca Cola, and I would drink up to six litres a day. I would crave it and if I went for more than a day without a "hit" I would start to experience withdrawals in the form of headaches, crankiness and just being an unpleasant human. I was both psychologically and physiologically addicted to the black gold. I still am addicted. On a physiological level, I was addicted to the caffeine and sugar hits, which my body relied on for an energy boost.

While it was no fun to experience the physical effects of going cold turkey on Coke, it was the psychological addiction that was the real tough one to break. I would use Coke as a reward, as a consolation, as a stimulant and as a refreshment. Graduated from my Masters? Celebrate with a Coke. Had a crappy day? Make myself feel better with a Coke. Feeling flat? Use Coke as a pick-me-up. Thirsty? Refresh with a Coke. I was a walking – OK, wobbling – advertisement for the company.

A habit is our mind's way of taking something we do regularly and automating it so we hardly even need to think about the elements that make up the skill. The more we do something, the more it becomes second nature, like riding a bike or brushing your teeth. But when we start to crave a habit or engage in it even though it's detrimental to us, it moves into the addiction category. Smoking, alcohol, sex, drugs, Coca Cola, sugar and even negative thoughts are some of the things we can become addicted to.

Often, the reason we become addicted to substances or activities is because they allow us to avoid much deeper psychological issues and pain. In small doses, many of these things are not inherently bad or damaging, but in excess they can become destructive.

To manage or change our addictions and habits to remove the self-harmful elements, it's useful to understand how habits work. At least some of the habits you built around your old normal will need to change, otherwise you won't be able to move forward confidently into the new normal. What habits are you addicted to in your old normal that no longer serve their purpose or will stop you from evolving? Write them down so you have a record of them and can review them as you move forward.

Remember: nothing changes if nothing changes.

THE STAGES OF HABITS

There are five stages that combine to create our habits and addictions, regardless of whether the habit is nose-picking, smoking or illicit drugs.

1 TRIGGER
2 CRAVING
3 ROUTINE
4 REWARD
5 REFLECTION

Stage 1: Triggers There is always something that kicks off a bad habit. Your trigger may be walking past a bar, waking up, boredom, being anxious about something new, or receiving bad or good news. Me? I'm a sucker for an ice-cold bottle of Coke, when I see it in the fridge the frosty condensation beckons me, which always leads to cravings and eventually me satisfying the urge. Smells, sounds, images or interactions with others can be the triggers that kick off a habit. There is usually not much we can do about triggers as they are simply innocuous things that we have learned to associate with habits or routines that feed our addictions. Psychologically, a trigger starts as a thought that seemingly comes from nowhere and just seems to grow in volume.

Stage 2: Cravings Once the trigger arrives, the associated routine, such as smoking or drinking for example, becomes all we can think about. The tricky part is that most of the time, what we crave is not the activity or routine itself, such as smoking, getting high or sex, but the feeling that goes with it, such as peace or relief from emotional pain. To avoid the harsh truth of what our addictions and habits are really hiding, *Bob* likes to mask them as routines that lead to temporary relief from the underlying cause.

Stage 3: Routine The routine is the action or series of actions we do in response to the craving. Smoking, getting laid, drinking, doing drugs: these may all form part of the routines we have created to satisfy our urges. Sure, abstinence may be an alternative to undertaking the routine, but if you're going cold turkey you'll need to replace the next stage with something else. *Bob* doesn't like to lose when it comes to our habits.

Stage 4: Reward The reward is the most significant part of this whole process. It's the one factor that will determine if we want to do it again and again. *Bob* will try to convince us that if the reward is only small then it's unlikely that our habit will transition into a full-blown addiction. Most of the time, drug addiction is not so much about the physiological high that the person experiences, but rather the relief from psychological or physical pain that the high provides. Often it's this relief that becomes the reward. We might feel more relaxed, calm, confident, valued or any one of the many positive feelings humans experience. Physiologically, when we have a positive experience, it releases a powerful hormone into our brains called dopamine, which reinforces the message that we enjoyed it. The problem with dopamine is that the more we have of it, the less sensitive our brains become to it, so *Bob* will encourage us to do the addictive behaviour more frequently to get the same dopamine hit.

Stage 5: Reflection As we bathe in the satisfaction of receiving our reward, the next stage that will hit is reflection. We may be savouring the pleasurable experience or enjoying the relief from our pain; our reflection could run the whole gamut from extreme joy to debilitating guilt. *Bob* doesn't really have a preference here because he can work with either reaction. If we're feeling guilty, *Bob* loves nothing more than to jump straight in, play the blame game and reinforce our shit. He might try to justify our actions, ignore them or reason with us that we could stop anytime if we wanted to (but there's no good reason to stop right now).

It's the power of these reflections that will eventually become the driver for us to break the habit cycle and take action. That may be today, tomorrow, next month, next year or never in some cases.

BREAKING HABITS

Breaking habits may seem really easy at first glance. The most obvious approach is to stop things before they start and attack the habit at the trigger stage. After all, just like a gun, if you don't pull the trigger the bullet won't fire and the rest of the cycle won't kick off. Simple: bad habit broken! Unfortunately, addiction doesn't work that way. For example, my Coke addiction would require me to avoid almost every fast-food outlet, petrol station or corner store if I were to avoid my triggers. Not exactly a feasible solution.

Once cravings hit they are a force that can't be reckoned with. *Bob* is looking for the reward and that's all he can focus on. It's like a two-year-old screaming for ice cream: there's no reasoning with them until they get their way.

Bob isn't giving up on the reward easily because this is what he has built much of the cycle on. The reward is what satisfies the cravings and what *Bob* is focused on achieving. However, often the reward is not what it appears on the surface. A drug addict might say that the reason they take drugs is to feel the high that goes along with it. But often when you dig deeper, you find that the high allows the person to escape their reality. At that particular time they're not suffering anxiety, depression or any other recurring negative thoughts that run on replay in their heads.

The reward they experience is not so much the high but rather calmness, peace and yes, feeling good. In the book *Shantaram*, partly based on author Gregory Roberts's life, the protagonist reveals how after suffering a painful divorce and losing access to his daughter, a friend introduced him to heroin. The character describes how he knew he was hooked as soon as it hit his blood stream. All the mental pain, hurtful self-talk and anxiety drifted away and for the first time in a long time, he felt at peace.

The reflection stage is unavoidable after indulging in your habit if there is some conflict in your head about it. Smoking, tubs of white chocolate ice cream, drugs, alcohol – we either bask in it because it gives us pleasure or beat ourselves up because, deep down, we know it's harmful. Of course, sometimes we do both. After an affair, you may reflect on the incredible sex but quickly become racked with guilt for betraying your partner. While reflections are a strong motivator for changing or reinforcing behaviours and thoughts, they're not a very useful place to try to break a habit as they occur after the horse has bolted.

This leaves us with routine. All the other stages are critical, as they provide us with the insights about what our real rewards are and why we're addicted to the habit. If we understand those components, we can start to introduce new routines to deliver the true reward *Bob* is seeking. For example, I am a sugar fiend. It's another of my addictions and I often indulge this habit during a workday, when I will duck out to the shop to grab a drink and a bag of sweets. If I break down the real reward I get from this habit, it's not satisfying hunger, and it's not the sugar hit (well, maybe a little). The real reward is that it breaks up the boredom of a long day at work or allows me to walk around. By pinpointing the real reward I'm looking for I can choose another routine that will address the boredom and stagnant feeling, such as a quick walk around the block, a chat to a co-worker or a phone call to a friend. All better routines than the unhealthy sugar hit.

The final trick to embed a new routine so it becomes a habit is to build a reward system around it. Alcoholics and drug addicts count their number of days clean – the bigger the number, the more at stake if they break their streak. Choose a reward that's relevant to you that is small enough to be achievable and yet big enough to matter when you reflect on it. The more it matters to you and the more you acknowledge your achievement, the more it will help you change the routine to one that is beneficial to you.

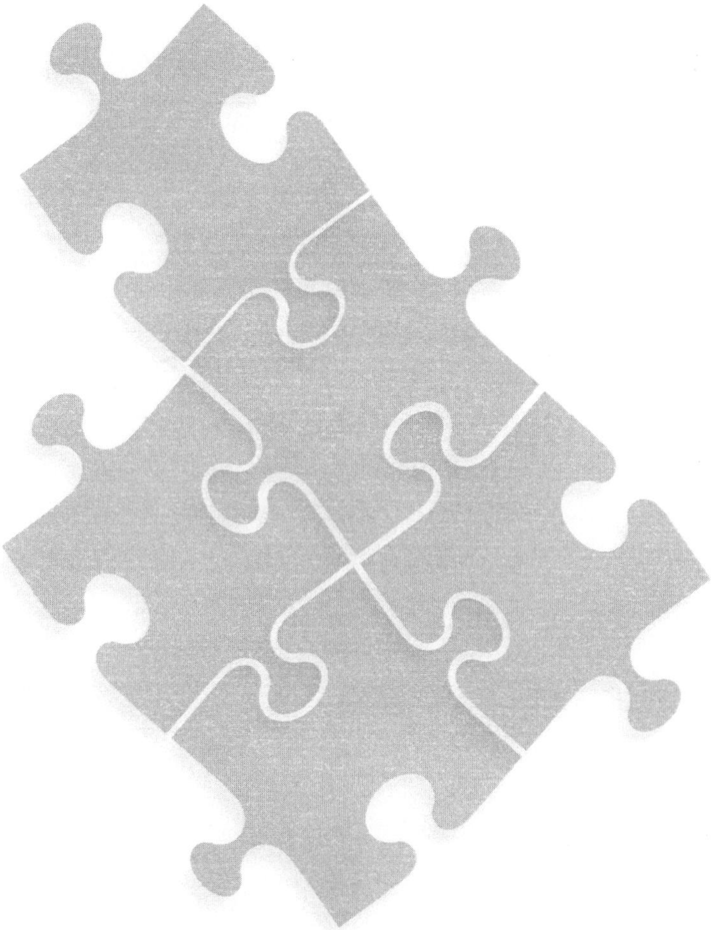

Stage 5: Try, then Try Again

"I've missed more than 9000 shots in my career. I've lost almost 300 games. Twenty-six times, I've been trusted to take the game-winning shot and missed. I've failed over and over and over again in my life. And that is why I succeed".

— Michael Jordan

STAGE 5: TRY, THEN TRY AGAIN

Keep chipping away

A close friend of mine, Tim Horan, used to play rugby union for the Australian team, the Wallabies. He played over 80 test matches for his country and was recognised as one of the best centres in the world in the 1990s, known for his attacking prowess, formidable defence and playmaking ability. Whenever I phone Tim to say hi and ask him how he's going, his inevitable response is always "just chipping away". I had heard the saying before meeting Tim, but I had never fully grasped its meaning. When I finally asked him about it, he explained to me his theory of life and how it related to the sport that took him around the world and saw him meet the Queen of England and Nelson Mandela.

"When you're out on the field playing rugby you're always looking for the big break," Tim told me. "But they're pretty rare and often need to be worked at to uncover them. What you have to do is play the best you can and keep chipping away at the defence of the opponents until that break appears, and when it does you grab the ball and run for it with everything you have."

Tim took his on-field approach of chipping away and used it to make a very successful career after sport as he reinvented himself in the corporate and commentating arenas. He knows that it's unrealistic to win every game or to expect that break will always come; rather you need to be prepared, keep working at it and grab opportunities with both hands when they do come up.

The previous sections of this book have been about getting ready and starting to take action. But as we all know, life comes with setbacks, diversions and challenges. These ups and downs are normal; what isn't normal is expecting that life will always be trending up and you will always get your way and win the game of life. All too often, the vision we created for our new normal and the plan we have to achieve it were built in a land where unicorns exist and rainbows are what they poop. In other words, the plan is set for the best-case scenario and ignores the reality that life is often a little messy.

This is when the mind games start. We know that any change or journey to a new normal means stepping outside our comfort zone and our success will be determined by several key attributes including commitment, determination, motivation and resilience. On one side is the current normal team, of which *Bob* is the captain, looking for any reason, real or perceived, to quit, give up, abandon or scamper away from the quest. On the other side is you and your vision of your new normal, with your well-thought-out plan leading the way. One team makes its plays based on fear and the other on its level of determination.

STAGE 5: TRY, THEN TRY AGAIN

Imagine the quest as a video game with many challenges and levels. As you play, if you fail, crash or even get killed you get the opportunity to restart at the beginning. Every time you start over you get to know the best paths to take and what to expect along the way. Each time, you learn something new about the game. When you succeed at one stage you're rewarded with access to the next level and the cycle repeats. Fail at the higher level and you have to start all over again.

Gamers can lose themselves in these side quests for days, even years. Here's the interesting thing: each time they lose and have to start over they're failing, but with each new try they're learning something new about themselves and the game. A gamer knows that you need to fail in order to succeed.

The restart in a game is a lot like life. Sometimes we think we'll only ever get one break and if we miss it, we should quit. But in reality, we're allowed many tries and we really only fail when we give up.

I have long been fascinated with what makes some humans more likely to quit and others keep going until their last breath. Sometimes these are extreme stories of survival, such as holocaust survivor Eddie Jaku, author of *The Happiest Man on Earth*, who kept going in the most horrific circumstances. I regularly question whether I could keep getting back up when faced with similar situations. What I've noticed in nearly any case of survival against the odds is the person's ability to clearly visualise themselves enjoying their new normal. The difference between a great life and an unfulfilling life is not how many times you succeed, but how you recover from your failures and setbacks to keep pushing forward.

Even in our everyday lives we constantly face challenges that test our resolve to keep trying or give up. If you've just started a new diet and someone offers you a piece of chocolate mousse cake, do you quit your goal for a short-term treat? No judgement here, I'm going for the cake every time. But if you're really committed to the goal, staying on track becomes easier. The more we say no and the more we start to hear people ask "Have you lost weight?" then the greater our resolve becomes.

The strength of our resolve is determined by several factors, including our commitment to our goal, how motivated we are to achieve it, our drive and determination to do what we need to get there, and our resilience in being able to get up and keep going when we hit setbacks. The other element that is key to our success is our ability to learn from our mistakes. As the saying goes, "Insanity is doing the same thing over and over again and expecting different results". There are really only two ways you can truly fail: the first is if you don't learn from your failures, and the second is if you give up.

By reframing our failures, we become more accepting that they are necessary (and yes, painful) steps in getting to where we want to be.

In the many examples of almost superhuman resilience you can find online when you dig into successful people's stories, you will find that the journey was longer than expected and they encountered many setbacks along the way. Every single story I have read about successful people includes some dark times filled with self-doubt and a moment in which they almost gave up, as well as details about the spoils of their successes. It's almost a rite of passage to achieving long-lasting success to have been tested along the way. On the other hand, when success is the result of the gods smiling on you, the enjoyment it brings is often fleeting. Research on lottery winners discovered that most felt their lives were worse following their windfall.

The strength of our resilience comes from a couple of elements. Some of us are just born stubborn, the kind of people who don't give up until they get their way. The rest of us conformed with what was expected of us and always tried to please others. Don't worry if, like me, you fall into the latter group, because the thing about resilience is that it's like any other habit. The more setbacks you experience, the more you learn about yourself and the game you're playing, and the more resilient you become.

When I feel like the world is against me and I'm at risk of giving up there are several steps I take to get back on track. You will note that the steps below are a micro set of the larger steps outlined for mastering reinvention. The reason for this is that each of the setbacks helps change you and sets you on a new path of reinvention.

Step 1: Acceptance. Accept that things haven't gone to plan and let go of the self-destructive emotions that could derail your next effort. Given I'm impatient, this process of acceptance usually incorporates a loud, animal-like growl of frustration accompanied with a few words that would have got my mouth washed out with soap in my childhood. If you let the failure get in your head it can become all-encompassing and stop you moving on. Just watch a tennis player when they screw up a shot. If they beat themselves up about it, that one missed serve or volley can determine the whole match.

Step 2: Recovery - Recovering from the setback can be difficult, but you need to find your way to a less emotional state where you can reflect without your perspective being overly tainted by anger, sadness, euphoria or any other emotions that *Bob* can use to stop you regrouping and trying again.

Step 3: Reflection - Review what happened, what you could do differently and what could lead to success. In other words, learn from your failures rather than trying to hide them or ignore them. As Thomas Edison said about his efforts in inventing the lightbulb, "I have not failed. I've just found 10,000 ways that won't work". Take a moment to reflect what the setback means for your goal as well. As you evolve and become stronger in response to setbacks, your goals may also evolve and change.

Step 4: Refocus. Armed with the new knowledge and skills you have gained from your successful failure you are now better equipped to try again. Refocus on your goal and the things standing in your way with your improved understanding, which could help you see things in a new light.

Step 5: Adapt. I will recite one of the mantras I mentioned earlier: Nothing changes if nothing changes. If what you did last time didn't show any signs of succeeding, then doing the exact same thing again will probably lead to the same result. Adapt, pivot or vary your approach to enhance your chance of success. By

STAGE 5: TRY, THEN TRY AGAIN

keeping a note of what you did and changed each time you can identify the things that failed or could help you succeed. Stay observant and avoid becoming despondent, as that is a certain pathway to quitting.

Step 6: Try again. Keep going, keep chipping away. You may not have found the gap or the break you need to take, but if you aren't even on the field then you never will. You only fail when you quit; all the other times you failed you have learned what doesn't work, bringing you one step closer to what might actually score your winning goal.

Oh, lastly and most importantly, tell *Bob* to STFU if he starts with any of the excusitis stuff he likes to throw at you to convince you to give up. He may try telling you that you are too old, too young, not smart enough, not educated enough or not pretty enough to do what you want. But remember, *Bob* is not in control, you are. So just thank him for his thoughts and get back to trying again.

Cover your bases

As I mentioned in the chapter "Let's bounce", prior to COVID-19 my wife and I had a startup called localyokl. When we travel we like to connect with locals to really experience the true essence of the place and, where possible, avoid the manufactured tourist traps.

One such experience happened while travelling through Nepal. I got chatting to a local man selling momos (the Nepalese version of a dim sum) and ended up being invited back to his family home for dinner. Everyone turned out to greet us – immediate family, neighbours, third cousins removed. They saw our visit as a real honour when in fact we were the ones who felt privileged to be able to connect on such a personal level. They watched in awe as we dined on their local food, which made it even harder to chew and swallow the tough-as-leather yak steak they had prepared. After dinner we taught the kids an Australian song called "Give Me a Home Among the Gumtrees", with the actions of course. There was much laughing, hugging and good times. It is a moment that is embedded in my memory for life.

Our vision for localyokl was to offer this kind of experience to everyone by providing a marketplace where locals and travellers could connect on a more personal level to share authentic experiences. It was like Uber but for travel experiences.

After we had been working on it for about 12 months and invested a few hundred thousand dollars in it, along came Airbnb Experiences with a similar offering. After the initial "oh, crap" moment we quickly realised that this would help legitimatise the market for us. People would be more accepting of the concept if there was a larger player also entering the market. On we went, doing multiple media interviews, talking to investors, winning government grants and envisaging becoming the next unicorn – that is, a startup valued at over $1 billion. They're called unicorns because out of the squillions of startups, only a very rare few reach those stratospheric heights. In my head we were well on the way.

Then two things happened. We ran out of money – we literally had nothing left, so I went back to consulting to earn money to keep us afloat until we could get investors on board. Then COVID-19 arrived to deliver the final fatal blow. Having spent every cent we had and every ounce of energy and motivation, I came away shattered, broke and very depressed. Success was so close, but it didn't play out the way I expected.

Picking up the pieces took some time, but I had experienced tough times before and knew I would come out the other side eventually. That's the good thing about experience: it gives you a platform to manage future challenges and disappointments from, also known as resilience. Once I started to emerge from the gloom, a few things happened. I wrote and published my first book, *Sort Your Sh!t Out*; I managed the delivery of the IT solution for Queensland's COVID-19 tracing program; I renovated our house with my wife; and I co-created another startup to help individuals better manage their personal risk for COVID-19 and other medical conditions. They're all things I wouldn't have done had localyokl not gone into hibernation.

Each time something doesn't go to plan – and it often doesn't – I follow the six steps outlined in the previous chapter to understand why it went wrong, what I could have done differently and what needs to change.

Sometimes, the reason it hadn't gone to plan was my plan wasn't well thought out to start with. I was blinded by my enthusiasm and the dream of the potential reward or payoff. In those situations I only have myself to blame. I didn't put the work in upfront to set myself up for success. Now with AI I have even less of an excuse for not doing my due diligence. Other times, the plan didn't play out as expected because the situation changed, other people didn't do their part, or there was a high degree of unknowns in the outcome because it was new territory that hadn't been explored before. If you're trying something new and unchartered, there is a higher chance that you'll need to try multiple times to find the way through, and that you'll fail along the way.

Investors talk about risk return as one of their key considerations. The higher the risk of the investment, the more an investor expects to be compensated for taking it on. I recently decided to throw some money into the crypto market, attracted by the stories of people who invested $20,000 and saw it grow to over $500 million. Because the return was so high and the market so volatile I knew I would be in for a ride and there was a chance I would lose everything I put in. As a result, when the market took a dive and my investment was halved I wasn't as shattered as I might have been had I thrown everything I had into it.

The stakes in our investments for our journey are determined by the importance we place on the outcome, the time we have available to achieve it, and whether we entered into it with our eyes open about the risks of failure involved, and how we would deal with that failure should it occur. There are a couple of strategies I have adapted from my business and transformation work which, when applied to one's personal journeys, helps avoid being defeated by failure.

Spreading the risk by diversifying is another strategy investment advisers like to use. It involves setting up a portfolio that maximises returns while helping to protect your interest without betting everything on one high-risk option. Putting everything into a high-risk strategy is the equivalent of gambling: great if it pays off, but the chances of winning are pretty low. Think about a few alternatives or options that you might have available to you to achieve your end goal or maybe even consider variations of your goal to explore. Now, don't think for a moment that I'm suggesting that you shouldn't be committed to your goal. Instead I'm saying to look at all the options you have available to you and don't forget to leverage AI to help you.

Once you have identified your options you can set off on one or maybe even several of them at the same time. This is the "fail fast and fail small" approach. You get to test the water to see how your plan stacks up and what you need to learn before you completely jump in. As a donut aficionado I sometimes dream about owning a chain of stores offering the best donuts imaginable. The most prudent way to approach achieving this dream would be to start small, cooking up some donuts at home and testing the demand at local markets; once I built a following I would find a site in a great location to open a shop; depending on how that went, I would then look to grow the business to become the czar of donuts globally. My dream hasn't changed throughout the journey, but this approach allowed me to avoid risking everything until I understood the risks and pitfalls.

With AI you can even leverage proven approaches other digital marketers have used to figure out where to focus their effort and marketing dollars to get the best return – or in our case, the best chance of success. Back to my donut empire. When I'm deciding on which donuts to put all my effort into making, I would consider what I would like and also chat to friends about what they would buy. All these insights are hypothetical; the real proof will be when we put them out for sale and discover which varieties sell the best.

In digital marketing they call this A/B testing. To test which advertisement or strategy they should focus on they will develop several alternative strategies to achieve their goal. Then they will invest the same small amount behind each one and see which gets the best results. They use their learnings from this real-world test

STAGE 5: TRY, THEN TRY AGAIN

to evolve their strategy and inform where to spend the majority of available dollars and effort.

One final thing to do is write stuff down as you go. Not only does writing down your thoughts and plans help clarify things, it forces you to consider the consequences in more detail and it acts as a journal you can refer to throughout your journey. The accuracy of our memory of events erodes over time. My dad and I have very different recollections about what happened on the night my mum passed away, and yet we were both there and experienced exactly the same tragic event.

Journalling gives you a record of where you started and what your goals are, as well as providing you with a way to capture your learnings and record what you have tried so you don't waste time doing the same thing again. The thing about *Bob* is his recollection of events, goals and strategies evolves as we move further along the path. This of course makes sense, but what it can do is diminish your understanding of how far you have come so that you forget to celebrate your milestones.

When things get tough, *Bob* may also try to convince you that your goals were more like "nice to haves" – optional rather than necessary – so that you compromise on reaching your full potential. From a personal perspective, journalling holds me to account for what I signed up to as well as provides a record for when people don't do the right thing or *their* version of events changes. Trust me, I speak from experience in this! When something starts to get legs and attracts interest from various parties you may find that your understanding and that of your trusted partners varies and can result in years of effort suddenly vanishing. Keep records of what you have signed up to and communicate clearly to the people you are relying on to ensure you achieve what you are looking to do.

Take note; just do it!

STAGE 5: TRY, THEN TRY AGAIN

Beware of comparisonitis

One of the delights of being a gruncle (great uncle) is being able to watch my nephew and niece go through their super cute stages as they develop and become toddlers. Toddlers are one of the true masters of reinvention as they are quickly adapting to the world they're in. They can learn multiple languages, explore with wonderment, and of course, one of the major milestones is learning to walk. As adults we watch with edge-of-your-seat anticipation as our mini humans try and try again to master the art of walking. There will be teetering, face plants, bum slams and one-legged balancing acts as their brain and body learn what works and what doesn't when it comes to the skill of walking. And we are there every misstep of the way as we encourage them with excited goos and gaas to keep going and keep trying. Eventually there's one step, then two steps, and hold back the tears and squeals, the kid is a genius – they are walking.

As we journey down the path we have chosen to travel we could learn a lot from how we support and encourage a toddler learning to walk. The goos and gaas may not be needed, but if we treated a toddler learning to walk to the same negativity and unfair comparisons we use on ourselves, their development would be set back considerably and their first steps would take far longer. Imagine if the first time a toddler tried to stand we said to them, "That's nothing special, Mable from next door started walking two weeks earlier." When they fell, instead of encouraging them to get back up, we yelled, "What is wrong with you? Are you stupid? Walking isn't that hard, nearly everyone can do it. Be better, kid!" Even worse, what if we punished them every time they failed to walk? You can imagine how messed up this kid would be. Sure, they would eventually walk, but just think of the size of the psych bills they'll have to cover in the future. And yet, this is how we let *Bob* treat us.

I see it in the gym all the time. People who have just signed up and haven't seen the inside of a gym for years walk in and look around at the people working out. All too often they will try to keep up with people who have been training for years, or in my case, decades. They have caught the very contagious comparisonitis, which is the very human habit of comparing our progress, attractiveness, intelligence and almost every other trait to others to see how we measure up. If *Bob* thinks we are outperforming others, we may brag or get a confident swagger about us. But if we don't feel like we're measuring up and don't believe we can compete, we may hide, get depressed and despondent, or just give up.

What *Bob* often misses when suffering a bout of comparisonitis is the backstory behind who and what we are comparing ourselves to. For example, if you're starting out in a new industry, comparing yourself to someone who has been training in the same arena for years is useless and dangerous. You simply haven't put in the time, experienced the failures, learned the lessons and tried again and again until you've mastered whatever it is you're working towards.

Of course, there is good and bad comparisonitis. Good comparisonitis pushes us to try harder and keep improving. For example, my wife and I regularly remind each other that "it isn't a competition" when one of us decides to do something that in turn inspires the other to do the same thing. It could be writing, exercise, yoga or watching a movie – anything. Because she's smarter than me (actually no, I'm smarter than she is ... see how it starts?), I'm not sure she doesn't just say she's going to the gym to bait me then goes to have coffee with the girls instead. Either way, I'm better off.

Bad comparisonitis sees us compare apples with oranges. For example, expecting that you can hold your own in a swimming race with an Olympic gold medallist, despite having only just recently jumped back in the pool. This type of comparison can be destructive to your motivation and commitment to your goals. It all comes down to what your expectations, mindset and goals were when you dived in. If it was to get a reality check on how much work you had to do to be competitive, then sure, get your ass whipped. With this attitude, the experience becomes an enjoyable and constructive learning opportunity or fan experience rather than an unrealistic expectation that you could beat them without putting in the work.

Your drive to keep pushing through the challenging times and failed efforts – and they will be there – will be dependent on your degree of motivation. External motivation from others who might be coaching or mentoring you is great, but the problem with external or extrinsic motivation is that you need to ensure that *Bob* will stay on your side when you experience a setback. When that external motivator isn't there and you're alone with *Bob*, your drive to keep going can be seriously undermined because your motivation to succeed is tied to impressing your coach or mentor rather than fulfilling your vision.

The best type of motivation comes from within. This internal or intrinsic motivation is the strongest kind because you're connected to it – you know what it is you're striving for and you're kind to yourself about your efforts to achieve it. Sure, top up your drive when you need to by turning to coaches, mentors or friends to encourage and motivate you. But don't kid yourself; you can't outsource your motivation and drive, just like you can't outsource your goals or doing the work to achieve them.

STAGE 5: TRY, THEN TRY AGAIN

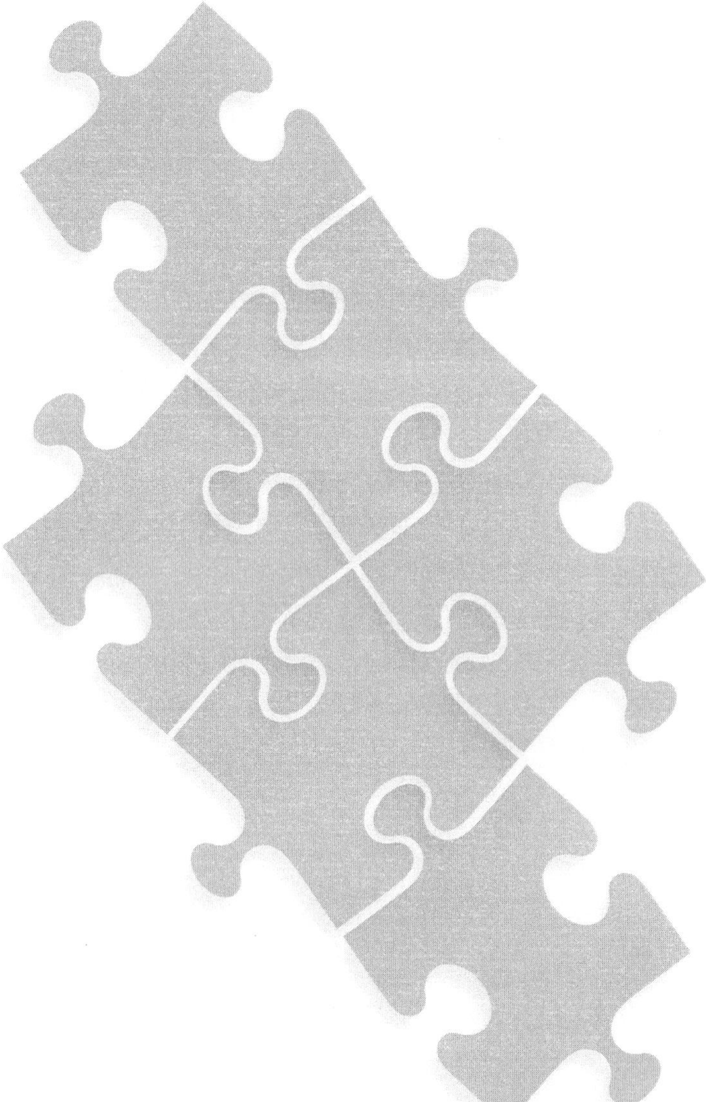

Stage 6: Enjoy the Journey

"Don't take life too seriously! Nobody gets out alive anyway. Smile. Be goofy. Take chances. Have fun. Inspire".

— Dawn Gluskin

STAGE 6: ENJOY THE JOURNEY

Be kind to yourself and others

One of the things Mum hated about her cancer was, surprisingly, not so much the cancer itself – because she realised it was coming from within her own cells so that would be a form of destructive self-hate – but rather the reactions of others. Ask any cancer survivor and they will probably have similar stories of how others change the way they interact with them on hearing about their illness. Mum was 48 when the doctors announced that they had to either amputate her leg or she had to accept a life expectancy of months rather than years or decades. Of course, there were no guarantees that the cancer wouldn't return, but amputation gave her the best chance of seeing her grandchildren grow older and meet those yet to be born. She was always a practical woman so she quickly weighed up the situation and agreed to go ahead with the amputation. Once the decision was made she stepped – well, more like hopped – into her new life.

There were many elements of Mum's new life that demanded she adjust: hopping on one leg, using crutches, spending over a decade searching for a prosthetic limb that allowed her to walk with the least limp possible. But there was one aspect that Mum could not and would not adjust to, and that was how others reacted to her bald head or the fact that she had one leg shorter than the other (her words). If you or someone you know has gone through cancer and chemo or some other sort of significant physical transformation, either good or bad, you will be able to relate.

People would approach Mum and talk to her in a sad, almost resigned tone that inferred that death was inevitable. As a gloriously stubborn and strong woman, this type of attitude would rile her up. In her mind, the only person who was going to decide whether the fight was over or not was herself, not some relative or colleague who she hadn't seen for years. Those death stares and funeral-home tones were never meant to harm – they were the reactions people would offer when they had no other way to express their emotions or had no experience to draw on when interacting with someone experiencing cancer. They may have been clumsily trying to support and console as they struggled to come to terms with the rawness of the situation. So, while it used to annoy Mum, she would always be kind and polite to them.

The other thing I admired about my mother was her wisdom and the empathy she had for others. While she had no time for people who would deliberately hurt or deceive others, she seemed to have endless understanding for those who were misguided or who just stuffed up. Her view was that these people were well intended and were unlikely to realise what they were saying or the potential

STAGE 6: ENJOY THE JOURNEY

impact of their words on her inner determination. So rather than get angry and correct them she would calmly engage with them and let their misguided attitude wash over her.

For the people who knew Mum BC (Before Cancer), her updated version sans leg and hair would have been a shocking contrast to their previous image of her. While Mum had time to grieve for her lost identity as a two-legged person as well as adjust to her new normal, the people seeing her again for the first time since the surgery had to rapidly update their image of her identity. Often, they had no time to adjust and grieve for the loss of the person they had known. Admittedly, they weren't the ones who had lost their leg, but their insensitive comments and reactions likely stemmed from shock as they grappled to connect the person they knew with the altered woman who stood before them.

The other hidden factors that affect how people will react to the new you and the journey you have been on is whether they agree with your choices, how they think they would have managed in similar situations, and the vibe you give off.

This is where your sphere of control comes back into play. You may not be able to control what others think, say or do, but you can control your reactions and actions as you process it. So, while how you've changed may be none of their business, nor are you interested in what they would have done, you can choose to acknowledge that some will say or do the wrong thing despite their best intentions. I know I struggle with finding the appropriate words when someone reveals a loved one has passed away. Do you say, "I'm sorry for your loss" or "I hope you're OK", as I have been known to blurt out? Neither is perfect, but really, there is nothing that I can say that will make the situation better. These days I ask how I can help, while still bumbling through some uncomfortable platitude. That way I'm at least offering to support the person as they adjust to their new reality.

Dinesh Palipana OAM is a lawyer who went on to study medicine and become an emergency doctor in one of Queensland's busiest hospitals. I had the privilege of interviewing him for this book and there were so many things that made our meeting special. Dinesh's intelligence, compassion, energy and generosity were what stood out to me. His ability to reinvent himself has been a lifelong journey, but what has stayed with me was his description of the reactions people had to him after the accident that made him a quadriplegic halfway through his studies.

As Dinesh phrases it, after the accident he lost everything. Not only did he lose the use of his limbs, he lost his family home as they struggled to pay the bills. But what was most surprising was that he also lost the support of his friends, and even his own father, as they struggled to relate to his new identity. The beautiful thing about Dinesh is that when he talks about these relationship losses you know that, while he still can't comprehend why those closest to him weren't there when he needed them, he has accepted that this is their burden to bear. He doesn't hate them, as this is not within Dinesh, but he recognises that they couldn't deal with the awkwardness of his transformation and he needed to keep moving forward and leave those who weren't supporting him to follow a different path.

If you are confronted by something negative, real or perceived, that could potentially impact your journey or your commitment and motivation to reach your goals, remember that it's within your power to decide how much you absorb and how much influence they have on your successful reinvention. You get to choose to receive these interactions with compassion and understanding and release them if they don't align with your vision, rather than taking them on board and letting them fester into bitterness, resentment and anger.

Being kind is about being kind to yourself as well as those who may be misguided in their comments and actions. If their actions lead to significant conflict within yourself, be kind to yourself and have the courage to let them go. Just because people may have been able to fit into your old life doesn't mean that there will be a place for them in your new world. Sometimes things change, people change, and your needs change. Don't feel guilty about letting go of the things that no longer fit. If you're truly committed to the new you then you need to surround yourself with people who align with your goals and support you with the same kindness you are willing to offer them.

It's natural to lose friends through life's journey: you change, they change, interests change – things just change. This is another experience you can apply the Marie Kondo method to, ensuring that you move forward with the least amount of guilt and regret for letting go. Recognise and appreciate the role these relationships played in making you who you are and then thank them (even just in your head) for their service before moving forward.

Some paths you will need to walk alone; on other paths you will find companions who will walk with you. They may stay with you only for small sections before their path diverges from yours. Your paths may cross in the future or may never intertwine again. Others may travel beside you for a long way on your path and together you may discover new and different paths. Be wary, though, if you find yourself always alone on your path, and never give up your own path for another without doing so with love and without regret or remorse.

If you don't learn to move past those who have done you wrong or failed to support you when you needed them, you're letting them continue to influence your life. This makes no sense. They did a pretty crappy job last time, so why would you continue to let them determine your future? If you decide that they have a part to play in your life going forward, you need to ensure they respect your journey and being.

Be kind to yourself because you deserve it and be kind to others because they may not know better, but you do. The great thing about showing kindness is that you get paid back many times over. If you're feeling down and help someone else in need, you both end up feeling better. I like to live by this mantra: in a world where you can be anything, be kind.

STAGE 6: ENJOY THE JOURNEY

Let yourself go

When I am completely stressed out with money worries, relationship stuff or just planning where my next reinvention will take me, instead of listening to *Bob* play the same track over and over again, I often choose to pack it all in and go surfing instead. It may seem that I am avoiding my fears – and you may be right. But sometimes, when you're overwhelmed and you can't find the way forward, contemporary neurological research shows that maybe the best way forward is to think about something else. Surfing is my thing and my wife's is horse riding; it doesn't matter what it is you choose to do – just lose yourself in whatever it is that brings you joy and calm.

As I paddle out through the surf I may have a head full of stuff that *Bob* is feverishly trying to work through, but once the first wave finds me it demands my complete and undivided attention. From that point on I'm focused on paddling out the back, looking for the next wave and trying to surf it the best I can. The weird thing is that I solve my most complex problems and have the best insights during these surfing sessions. I'm constantly fascinated that the best way to solve something is to stop focusing on it and give yourself a break.

It's as though *Bob* has been stressing so much that he's got himself worked up into a frazzle, and as a result I end up trying too hard. Surfing is like my pressure valve. It lets off the steam and allows *Bob* to chill out, look at things differently and find new ways of solving whatever problem had been stressing me. Then eureka brilliance overcomes me and I find myself saying, "Of course! Why didn't I think of that before?" The reason is that there was simply no room in my head.

To make room and release the pressure that has built up from the stress we put on ourselves there are some simple things you can do. Laugh, chill, connect and have fun to give yourself the best chance of succeeding and finding your way through. At the very least you'll enjoy yourself rather than wallow in your own darkness and negativity.

FIND YOUR HAPPY PLACE

If you ask people what their ultimate life goal is, most will say they want to live a happy and healthy life. Cultivating a mental "happy place" and visiting it regularly is certainly a good contribution to a fulfilled life. But searching for everlasting happiness is a dream that life all too easily disrupts. It's unrealistic to expect that every minute of every day can be filled with Disneyland-style joy and happiness. Yet, when things aren't going well, *Bob* often tries to convince us the whole universe is against us and, as a result, we can end up with a negative mindset, expecting life to be filled with bad things. When things are going well, instead of being able to enjoy them, *Bob* warns you not to get too caught up enjoying the moment, because it will change and you will be disappointed. This black hat approach to life may prove to be right half the time, but it also means that you miss out on enjoying the good times while you're waiting for things to turn.

There is enough serious shit to deal with in life without making up our own or using small and insignificant things that didn't go our way as evidence that our entire lives are crap. The people who are most content are those who approach life with a positive outlook and find joy and happiness in everyday moments. It really comes down to the one thing you can control: your outlook. And just like most things that involve *Bob*, maintaining your outlook is a habit. Similar to goal setting, start small and look for the positives around you. They are there, you just need to start looking for them.

"Life can be beautiful if you make it beautiful," noted Eddie Jaku, holocaust survivor, in his book *The Happiest Man on Earth*. Having survived the horrors of the holocaust, Eddie made a conscious decision to honour those who didn't make it. "I made the promise that from that day until the end of my life, I would be happy, polite, helpful and kind. I would smile," he wrote.

Like Eddie, you are in control of your choice to smile, find happiness in each day and enjoy your life. The thought patterns that lead you into dark, negative places can be interrupted if you recognise the symptoms early and have an action plan to break the cycle. It may be as simple as learning to laugh at your own misfortunes or seeing the beauty around you and appreciating the things you love about the people who matter. Yoga and daily meditation are also great tools for resetting your brain patterns to be present, slowing the world down and appreciating life.

LAUGHTER IS THE BEST MEDICINE

When you're going through challenging times, it can be hard to see the light for all the dark that's demanding your attention. You may be worrying about what the future holds or continuing to replay the past, and *Bob* is doing a job on you. Sometimes the best stress relief is just to laugh and have fun. I can hear the naysayers reprimanding me, "There are some situations where it's not appropriate to laugh", and they may be right. But I know when Mum came home from hospital without her leg, we found something to laugh about; when she was lying on her deathbed we shared many a laugh; and when my ten-day-old niece was in ICU with meningitis, we laughed. And boy, did we need to laugh! We needed relief from the horrible, harsh reality we were living through.

Call it gallows humour, poor taste or bad timing, but sometimes laughing is just the thing needed to break the tension and pressure of what we are experiencing. Often the people who end up surviving the most extreme situations are those who can stay positive and enjoy sharing a laugh with others. Here are some of the scientific reasons for getting your giggle on in both challenging and good times:

STAGE 6: ENJOY THE JOURNEY

- Laughing breaks your negative or stressed-out thought patterns and gives you room for more positive perspectives.

- It turns off the stress hormones, such as cortisol, which can cause long-term damage, and releases feel-good hormones such as serotonin.

- Laughing boosts your mood and may help to reduce depression and anxiety.

- It makes you more attractive to others socially, which helps build connections with others.

- It may build your immune system by increasing immune cells and infection-fighting antibodies, thus improving your resistance to disease.

- It changes your outlook on your situation and the world by letting some light through.

- Research has found that laughing combats heart disease and stroke risk by delivering oxygen to your heart, lungs and muscles and lowering blood pressure.

- Some studies have shown it relieves psychological and physical pain by releasing feel-good endorphins into the body; laughing is used in recovery therapy for addicts to help them move past the pain that has a hold over them.

- It helps you live longer. Research out of Norway found that people with a strong sense of humour have a lower risk of death from all causes.

- It helps you process some of the illogical shit you have been hanging on to.

To help you get a daily dose of laughing medicine, switch on some comedies, read and tell dad jokes (yes, they are funny and I will take the laugh regardless of whether you are laughing with me or at me), hang out with funny and weird people, be silly or just throw a costume party for no reason. Whatever it takes to get your laugh on!

STAGE 6: ENJOY THE JOURNEY

Do good sh!t

I was walking past a café the other day, checking out the décor and trying to see what the food was like, when I saw a woman sitting at a window table, slowly stirring her coffee and writing in a notebook. While her food looked OK, she obviously was not. She was crying – almost sobbing – as she tried to compose herself.

Seeing someone in distress triggers my Superman complex as my wife calls it, which is when I need to try to fix things and make people feel better. It doesn't matter if the person in distress is male, female, old or young, if I can think of something that might make them feel better, I will do it. Help load a car for an elderly person? I'm there. Flat tyre? Pass me the jack. Lady sobbing in a café? I don't want to intrude so I go to the counter and pay her bill. It didn't matter that she wasn't aware I paid the bill; in my head all I wanted to do was help a stranger in a time of need and let her know someone cared.

I certainly didn't do it looking for her gratitude, as I quickly walked away before she knew what I had done to avoid any awkwardness.

Call it paying it forward, being kind or just helping others, I walked off to continue my shopping, feeling better about myself and the world. The thing about doing good shit for others is that it does seriously good shit for you too. Before you start to think I'm talking myself up as this wonderful guy, let me tell you, there are lots of things about me that balance out the do-gooder stuff. Even when it comes to doing good shit I'm being selfish, because I get more out of it than I give.

The reason people like Bill Gates, Warren Buffett and many anonymous others give away large chunks of their fortunes is not for the public recognition. Yes, sometimes there's an agenda to try to sway public opinion, but in the majority of cases they do it because they want to help those less fortunate. But the psychology of giving is much more selfish than it appears. I'm not trying to spoil the magic of charity and giving, just help you understand the real personal benefits you get back in return.

Remember that *Bob* has a very narrow view of the world and only cares about what's in it for us. Here's the great thing about doing good shit: everyone wins. It's definitely a two-way transaction. The subject of your goodwill gets help when they really need it, but you also get a release of endorphins, the feel-good hormones. There is a great term for this warm, fuzzy feeling: it's called the helper's high. Yes, you actually get a high, and like other highs, *Bob* notices and wants more of it. This can lead you to becoming "addicted" to doing good shit.

Like having a laugh, there is research confirming real, long-term health benefits associated with giving and helping others. For

STAGE 6: ENJOY THE JOURNEY

instance, it can reduce blood pressure, stress and the impact of the stress-related hormones, which can mean a longer, happier and more fulfilled life. The other biggie is that helping others helps your own self-esteem, which can lead to a clearer head and improved mood. Helping others distracts *Bob*, which means you are less focused on your own shit and as a result, you're better able to keep things in context.

There is, of course, a catch to doing good shit, and that is related to what you're looking to get out of it. If you give hoping for external recognition of your good deeds, you'll be disappointed, because not everyone on the receiving end is in a position to show their appreciation. The best type of motivation for giving is (again) intrinsic, where the buzz you get from knowing you have done good is enough of a reward.

Lastly, remember that doing good shit out of obligation is not the same as doing it because you want to or just because it feels good. If the reason is external, you may still feel the benefit of helping others, but if you're being pressured or guilted to help, *Bob* won't get the same buzz and you may end up feeling resentment or anger for doing something you didn't want to do. While ideally you will be able to get *Bob* to recognise that doing good shit is a win–win, if you notice that he's still dragging his feet and bringing everyone down with his negativity, then keep in mind that you are in control of the choices you make. You can choose not to do it or even better, look for the positives in what you're doing so that it isn't a waste of time. Then, selfishly, you'll get the helper's high you deserve.

Conclusion

Having reinvented myself more than 45 times through my different jobs, two marriages, identity crises, failures and successes one may think that I have mastered reinvention. Partly this is true. Yes, I have mastered the process of reinvention by the sheer fact I have done it so many times. The challenge remains though that for many of my future life-changing events I have never had to stare them down and respond. They haven't happened yet and will differ significantly from those I have faced in the past, otherwise I could just dust off the play book I used last time.

With such a rapidly changing world it is critical to master the *art* of reinvention. Art is in the eye of the beholder and will naturally be influenced by how the artist sees the world, the skills and tools they have available to them and how evolved their skills are. While change is inevitable, reinvention should be intentional as we approach life-changing events. Throughout this book, we've explored the transformative power of reinvention, especially in the face of challenges and uncertainties. With life constantly evolving, and it's up to us to shape the future we want, rather than simply reacting to the world around us.

STAGE 6: ENJOY THE JOURNEY

One of the biggest hurdles we have to overcome is our own fears, perceived identity and self-imposed limitations and beliefs. This is where *Bob* comes in trying to protect us, which often can result in us freezing or fleeing rather than fighting by amplifying our fears. Fear is about what could happen in the future, while those events that have already happened will demand our immediate response. We can't change the past, but we should definitely learn from it to avoid making the same mistakes over and over again. Yes I speak from experience here.

The world is changing at a rapid pace, with AI turning the dial up even further, and it's crucial to recognise that reinvention is the only positive option available to us to remain relevant. Hopefully the changes don't involve making drastic changes all at once. Reinvention should be about creating the best version of yourself through continuous learning, adaptation, and self-reflection. It's about being clear about your core values, your goals, and your vision for the future to enable you to CREATE meaningful reinvention.

Understanding how *Change* impacts us and our response to change helps us avoid overreact or become debilitated by the fear of the future. Not letting *Bob* take control helps us move forward into undertaking a *Reality check* of the situation, ourselves and the options available to us. Armed with this assessment we are able to start *Empowering* ourselves to take *Action* to adapt and succeed in our new world. Given we are stepping into the unknown we may experience false starts and even feel like we are slipping backwards, but it is through our resilience and persistence that we will be prepared to *Try, then try again* until we find our footing to start functioning and thriving in our new world. Given the level of discomfort we are likely to experience throughout this reinvention process one critical element is to enjoy the journey as much as we can.

Reinvention should be a conscious, deliberate choice – a decision to change, adapt, and grow, no matter the circumstances. This journey of reinvention is especially critical today, as we face shifts in every corner of our lives. From societal transformations to personal challenges and the rise of AI, we are living through a time of generational change. Many would argue that AI is the biggest challenge we are facing but try telling that to someone who has just won lotto, been diagnosed with cancer or had their heart broken. The need to manage and reinvent is not just about preparing for the future impacts of AI, rather it is about preparing ourselves to be ready for the more immediate changes we are facing.

As AI reshapes industries, revolutionises how we work and alters how we interact with the world, we must learn to adapt to it. AI is not just a technological shift; it's a cultural and personal one. It's one of the many changes that are transforming our landscape, making it all the more essential for us to redefine ourselves and our paths forward.

But here's the good news: just as you have adapted to every significant change in your life, you have the power to adapt to this one too. In fact, AI can be a powerful ally in our journey of reinvention. Used wisely it is not about replacing us, but about amplifying our potential. AI offers us tools to learn faster, work

STAGE 6: ENJOY THE JOURNEY

more efficiently, and even improve our well-being. The key, however, is to use it intentionally – just as we would any tool – in ways that serve our personal growth and future vision.

Using AI as a tool can help you but it should never overshadow your unique human qualities. Your creativity, emotional resilience, and capacity for growth are what make you irreplaceable. AI can amplify these qualities, but only if you actively choose to use it for your benefit.

So, where do we go from here? The future is open, full of possibilities, but it's not about the future "happening to you". It's about *you* intentionally creating the life you want in response to those changes. Reinvention is not a one-time event, it's an ongoing process that evolves with us as we learn, grow and adapt. Just as AI will continue to evolve, so will we. The key is to stay intentional about how we adapt to these changes.

The changes happening in the world are inevitable. We can't stop them, and we wouldn't want to. But how do we respond to them? That's where we have power. Reinvention is about aligning your life with the changes around you while staying true to who you are. The future is waiting for those who will seize this opportunity for personal growth. It's up to you to choose how you will respond to the changes that AI and other shifts bring. The future is ours to create.

Masters of Reinvention

"The truth is that our finest moments are most likely to occur when we are feeling deeply uncomfortable, unhappy, or unfulfilled. For it is only in such moments, propelled by our discomfort, that we are likely to step out of our ruts and start searching for different ways or truer answers".

— M. Scott Peck

When I am lost or looking for inspiration in times of uncertainty or significant change, I look for direction from people or mentors who have faced and mastered similar situations before. As part of researching for this book I interviewed many people and have included three of these reflections to highlight successful mastery of reinvention.

Angie Simpson

SINGLE MINDED

Angie and I had been trying to catch up for months to chat about what qualifies her as a Master of Reinvention. Every time I tried to make a suitable time, she was busy – and understandably so. It turns out that the reason Angie wasn't available was that she had recently separated from her husband and was in the process of reinventing herself as a single woman.

Never heard of Angie Simpson?

Angie is a woman of amazing strength, talent and determination. She swam for Australia in her younger years, and is now a qualified psychologist, author, producer and reality TV star, as well as mum to three overachievers: Cody, Alli and Tom. She also manages their careers, and, looking at the success they have had, she does a great job of that too. When Cody Simpson was "discovered" on YouTube playing covers of songs as well as his own compositions,

Angie and her husband packed up 13-year-old Cody and the rest of the family and moved to LA to record his first album. As Angie tells it, they knew it was a risk but she also knew that this was a once-in-a-lifetime adventure for not only Cody, but the whole family. So, they packed up and went on the road – true rockstar style.

She has fond memories of travelling on tour with her family and credits it with forming a strong bond between her three children. Alli and Tom have also had great success in the competitive world of television, music, acting and theatre. Angie's outlook and willingness to explore and reinvent herself is a trait she has passed on to her kids. In 2019 Cody decided to go back to his original passion and reinvented himself as a competitive swimmer, only narrowly missing out on booking a ticket to the 2024 Olympics. Damn underachievers!

When Angie and I did finally chat, she seemed slightly bemused as to why I wanted to talk to her. Like all the Masters of Reinvention featured in this book, there isn't one thing that makes her a master; it's a combination of life experiences and of course, her outlook. Masters like Angie may have become known for one element that brought them fame, however, like most so-called one-hit wonders, their success is a result of years of effort, filled with highs and equally-defining lows.

The details of Angie's separation were still raw when we talked and of course, this isn't the place for sharing that personal story. But what did come across was a person at a crossroads. She had made the decision that the life she had was no longer the one she wanted for her future, and she was exploring where single life would take her. Anyone who has been through a relationship breakdown knows that moving on involves grieving for what you've lost as much as finding a new path forward.

The catalyst for Angie was when she realised that she was caught in an unhappy and negative place in her life and it wasn't where she wanted to stay. She felt she deserved and wanted more and set about making changes to live the life she envisioned. Like all her previous life-changing decisions, this was not made on a whim. It involved lots of tears and self-reflection.

Angie has achieved so much in life, and I was struck by her willingness to be open and honest about where she was. She shared that her unhappiness had built up to a tipping point, or as she eloquently put it, "fuck this". Once that catalyst had taken seed, she set about changing her world by breaking ties with her old normal and exploring what reinvention looked like. It was emotional, sad and freeing at the same time, as Angie tells it. While Angie is still in the early stages of reinvention, I left with the knowledge that she would master whatever she did next, because she knows that you need to take a chance to get to where you want to be; you need to put one foot after another and work hard to make your goals and dreams a reality. The lessons from swimming continue to serve her well.

The key points I took away were:

- Maintain a positive outlook even in the face of adversity.

- Continue to adapt and flex when the world changes: opportunities can come from the most unexpected places.

- Life will always continue to evolve and change.

Tony Nash

TURNING NEGATIVES INTO SUPERPOWERS

Tony Nash is the co-founder and former CEO of Booktopia, an Australian startup that took on the global juggernaut Amazon in selling books online. At its height, it sold one book every 4.6 seconds. But Booktopia came from humble beginnings, rising out of the ashes of another failed startup. Coming off the back of failure meant the founders had to quickly pivot to be able to earn money just to put food on the table for their families.

Tony is someone whose drive, tenacity and success I have long admired from afar. Now, after talking to him, I also love his ability to turn negatives into superpowers and his capacity for reinventing himself. His story starts long before Booktopia when he achieved a pass mark of 56% in his Higher School Certificate. Somehow, Tony found himself in university, majoring in playing Space Invaders, he proudly notes. University only lasted six months before Tony realised the traditional education path was not for him. Like many of us, his early failures impacted him significantly and, despite all his success, he recognises they still form part of his motivation to prove he is "good enough".

After dropping out of uni, Tony started working for a large national company as the mail boy. Tony describes this as the predecessor to emails, as his job was to physically deliver messages from one person to another in the building. During this experience he realised he had a love for people, which he leveraged to venture into a career in IT recruitment. Around the same time, he discovered a passion for self-development, which has become a lifelong journey of working on himself and continually challenging his beliefs, values and behaviours through constant learning.

In the 90s, Tony, his brother and his brother-in-law saw an opportunity to build their own recruiting business, which they eventually sold to focus on their next startup – chat software that would allow businesses to communicate with their customers more effectively. They put everything into it and had global domination on their minds, as they were buoyed by the dotcom boom. However, like many booms, it was followed by a devastating bust, and sure enough, Tony and his siblings were left with nothing when the crash came.

Tony tried to rustle up new business for their software. He was presented with a seemingly random opportunity by the owner of a houseboat business. She was less interested in chatting to her existing customers than she was in attracting more customers to her website. Pivoting, Tony offered to help get her business to the top of Google's search rankings for $500, based on knowledge he had picked up from a passing conversation he'd had with a web designer a couple of weeks prior.

After that came better-paying contracts helping more companies with their digital marketing, frantically learning the ropes along the way to make sure they could deliver on their desperate promises. One of those customers would eventually change their future and fortunes. They were engaged to work with book retailer Angus & Robertson, which led to an introduction to another company that managed the marketing for 80 bookstores. This is when Tony came to the realisation that they too could start an online bookstore and from there, Booktopia was created.

When we think about successful people, we often just see the linear trajectory to glory, which is only the veneer of their story and who they are. This was true for my perception of Tony before I met him. Like any good story, his has many highs and lows. There has been good fortune, but it's his willingness to pivot and reinvent himself along the way that really defines him. His failures were hard lessons, but because he refused to give up they led to further opportunities, which he wouldn't have found without surviving the tough times.

While chatting, Tony revealed that he was diagnosed with a condition called attention deficit hyperactivity disorder (ADHD) four years ago. He has come to recognise it as his superpower. When his wife suspected he might have ADHD he went to his doctor only to be told that there was no way he could have it. "Look at how successful you are," the doctor reasoned. But after Tony's wife joined him at the next consultation and described his behaviours and focus, the doctor quickly agreed and prescribed the appropriate medication.

Tony described how entrepreneurs, artists or businesspeople with ADHD often appear passionate about what they do and seem obsessed and focused. Tony believes ADHD is his superpower because his ability to focus so intensely allows him to achieve superhuman feats. But like any unmanaged superpower, it comes with some downsides.

"People think you're incredible and accomplished, but it comes from these origins of just doing what you really want to do, and often this comes at the expense of everything else, including your relationships at home," he said. "Once diagnosed and treated, my relationships improved. I found that the things my wife used to nag me about became more obvious to me and I looked at them and saw that they needed to get done. I realised she wasn't nagging me, she was just communicating what still needed to be done."

Understanding his strengths and weaknesses was the pivoting point for Tony to reinvent himself once again.

Given Tony's connection to the book industry, it seemed fitting to wrap up our chat with a wordplay game. The first word was "intuition".

Tony started, "Intuition is made up of the words 'in' and 'tuition'. Tuition is a fee you pay to do something, such as learning something new. When things happen in your life you're in training to help you in the future."

The next was "reinvention". "Re means 'again' and invention relates to you inventing something new and hopefully more appealing," Tony riffed. "Mastering the art of reinvention is all about creating new things and discovering new paths."

I knew my intuition was on the mark when I asked Tony to be a Master of Reinvention – or maybe his superpowers extend to mind control and it wasn't my choice after all. Since this chat, Tony and Booktopia have experienced some challenging times but given his ability to adapt and flex I have no doubt he will come through this next stage changed, but successful. Regardless, the key points I took away were:

- Our life journey is never linear, there will be ups and downs.

- Learning is a lifelong journey – never stop working on reinventing the next version of yourself.

- Keep your eyes open, even when you're down, as the next opportunity may be just around the corner.

- With the right mindset you can turn your negatives into your superpowers.

Dr Dinesh Palipana OAM

OUR LIFE IS BIGGER THAN US

When it comes to mastering life-changing reinventions, I think Dinesh is up there with the best of them. His life story is peppered with significant events that by themselves may have broken the strongest of us, but for Dinesh they were lessons that made him stronger, more focused and more giving. He has survived wars, studied to become a lawyer, become a top ER doctor, and is recognised as an advocate for the rights of people with disabilities. He has received many awards for his dedication and commitment to making the world a better place and I certainly left our catch-up feeling honoured to have had the opportunity to meet him.

When I met him at the arranged spot I was slightly nervous. I went to shake his hand and totally messed it up and ended up doing some sort of awkward hybrid fist bump/high five/handshake, which we both pretended never happened, but more about that later.

Dinesh's story starts in Sri Lanka, where he was born in a time of much civil unrest. While the average Australian ten-year-old feels stressed if the internet goes down, Dinesh witnessed his neighbours being killed, burned alive with flaming tyres hanging around their necks. His family escaped, migrating to Australia in 1994 and finding peace and safety first in Sydney, and then in Byron Bay. This was before the Hemsworths made Byron even more famous – instead of A-listers, it was a home for chilled-out hippies. Dinesh really connected with Byron. It helped him recover from the horrors he had survived as well as start the journey of defining the type of man he would become.

Like many migrants, Dinesh was an overachiever who excelled at school, and he went on to study law in Brisbane. Despite his initial dream of becoming a highly paid mover and shaker in the world of law, something about it didn't sit right with him. He describes becoming disillusioned with what he saw as the materialistic focus and arrogance of the profession. The impact of this misalignment of values led to him experiencing a mental breakdown. While he didn't drop out, most of his final year of law studies was completed in the darkness of his mind and within the safe confines of his house. He was suffering serious anxiety and depression because of the internal conflict he was experiencing.

Now convinced that law wasn't right for him, Dinesh found himself at a crossroads, uncertain about what to do with his life, so he applied and was accepted to study medicine. It's interesting how often our inner values, and what we think we should do, come into conflict. And when we become open to acknowledging the disconnect, that's when we find our true purpose. This was what

Dinesh found with medicine. From the day he started medicine he realised this was what he was meant to do; helping others was his calling. He found his energy returned and the darkness left him as he passionately followed his vision. He was studying something he loved and had a great group of friends and an active social life. Life was good – actually, life was great ... until it wasn't. In 2010 his dreams came to a halt after a devasting car crash.

Dinesh recalls waking in hospital and the sheer horror and despair he felt when he realised he couldn't move his toes; he couldn't feel anything below his neck. He was paralysed. His life and identity were brutally changed. He went from being someone with a fully functioning body to a quadriplegic who was told his future as a doctor was no longer possible. The monsters of darkness returned; Dinesh found himself lost in a deep depression. After seven months in hospital Dinesh was released into a world he no longer recognised.

Despite still being the person he had always been, Dinesh found people were now treating him differently and surprisingly, many were actively avoiding him. The accident not only took away his functioning limbs – his whole world changed. Over the following years as he adjusted to the changes in his body, he and his mum lost everything. The house had to be sold to pay for his rehabilitation, his friends stopped coming around, and his dad left the family after struggling to cope with the loss of the son he had known. Dinesh doesn't talk about these losses with bitterness or hate, but rather with a sad understanding that his friends and father also struggled to adjust to his new identity and unfortunately, found it easier to avoid him completely.

However, there was one constant through the highs and many lows: Dinesh's mum. Having met her, I can tell you she is a courageous and strong woman and there was no way she would have ever let her son give up. He was still the person she knew and loved and with her by his side *they* started to find their way back to a new life.

The adjustment to his new identity wasn't an easy one. It took Dinesh a long time before he could look at himself in a mirror. He didn't want to be confronted with the identity of the person he saw. As he learned to accept and embrace his new identity he was once again able to check whether the Dinesh staring back at him had something stuck in his teeth after eating an orange and poppyseed muffin.

Sitting at the coffee shop after that awkward handshake, Dinesh shared with me how the accident had forced an awakening on him. As Dinesh pointed out, "Life's nice things and possessions may bring temporary joy, but life is transient and ever moving and those material and external things can be quickly ripped away without warning."

In a world where "new normal" and "old normal" form part of our everyday vernacular, Dinesh challenged whether "normal" existed at all, pointing out that as individuals, our lives and what we consider normal is as unique as our DNA. Dinesh went on to share how, in his experience, we become attached to external things, which can be changed and altered without our approval or input. This attachment to things, people and even our physical body can be disrupted at any time. Life is transient, as our journeys often show. What is normal today may vastly differ from what is normal tomorrow. Life's only certainty is that things will change.

Once his rehabilitation had returned adequate movement to his hands and he had mentally adjusted to his new identity, Dinesh decided that there was no reason not to continue working in medicine. He fought to be accepted back into his course and upon graduation, the fight continued. Despite qualifying as a doctor he was confronted with a new challenge. He couldn't get a placement in a hospital to complete his residency. "How can a quadriplegic be a doctor?" was the response he received to his applications. Not one to give up, Dinesh took his quest public and with the support of the media, in 2017 he was accepted by the Gold Coast University Hospital. He went on to become their junior doctor of the year in 2018. Dinesh has since co-founded Doctors with Disabilities Australia and runs research projects in spinal cord injury, including investigating how AI could reduce barriers for people with disabilities. He has also been admitted as a lawyer, which he plans to use in advocating for the rights of people with disabilities.

If I had to choose one thing that really personifies Dinesh, it wouldn't be his amazing resilience nor his ability to continually reinvent himself, or even his many inspiring achievements. The trait that I replayed in my head as I drove home that night was his beautiful and generous soul. His inner beauty really struck an emotional chord as he shared his vision that life is much greater than individuals or the things that happen to us. Dinesh reminded me that we all can do so much more, and the benefits we get from helping others far outweigh the material possessions we seek.

He is led by an unfaltering inner belief that our lives are bigger than just us and the greatest humans throughout history were focused on making the world a better place for everyone, not just what was in it for them.

As we wrapped up our chat I sincerely thanked Dinesh for his time and openness in sharing his story, and in his true humble style he was equally sincere in thanking me for taking an interest in what he had to say. I drove home reflecting on the power of what he had shared and the beauty and strength of this man.

My key Master of Reinvention takeaways from Dinesh were:

- Why let someone else dictate your life? Don't give up, fight for what you want.

- Always be willing to adapt and find ways to make things work.

- You will get more from your life by giving rather than taking.

- Always look for the things to be grateful for. They are there, they just may not be obvious straight away.

Acknowledgements

Thank you for entrusting Mastering the Art of Reinvention as a guide to help you on your journey to reinventing the next version of you. I sincerely appreciate it and feel honoured. Every author includes so much of themselves into their books and this book is no different. My writing is a snapshot of my life at that point in time based on the challenges and experiences that led me to that point. After my first book *Sort Your Sh!t Out* I was inspired to write this sequel by the stories from readers about how it helped them change their lives for the better. I was humbled and honoured to help so many people.

Firstly, the person I am today is a culmination of the all the events and people they have experienced. While I may not have mentioned the roles they played in my life, I would like to thank you for how you helped shape my life.

I owe a huge thankyou to Dr Dinesh Palipana and Craig s who honoured me by writing the forewords for Mastering the Art of Reinvention. These two gentlemen inspired me from the day I met them and make me a better person just by knowing them. Tim Horan is someone I think of as a lifelong mate, who just happens to be a former Wallaby. While his wisdom graces the pages in this book he also inspires me in my everyday life. He is always there to connect me with someone who can help with the next project or just to catch up for an almond cappuccino.

My beautiful wife Azra is a huge inspiration in my life. She lives her life with a huge heart and an unbridled passion and determination for her loved ones and is driven to becoming the best version of herself she can be. She is an accomplished author who has such a beautiful way with words that she inspired me to find my voice as an author. She is also the founder of Biohackher, super competitive and has a pathological fear of missing out, better known as FoMO. She holds me to account for my actions and pushes me to reinvent myself especially when I try to make excuses and avoid doing the work. In return, I amuse her endlessly with my self-classified hilarious dad jokes, boy brain bloopers and stuff ups. A pretty fair trade, I think.

Family plays an important role in my life and for me has a very broad definition. Firstly, there is my dad and his partner Gisela who are going as strong today, as they were in their younger days. Dad, at 83 is an inspiration and influence in so many ways. He stays as active today as he did in his youth, whether it be flying his plane around Australia or getting up onto a hanger roof to help a mate with repairs. Then there is my sister Sandra and her partner Marty who are just caring and giving souls.

My nephews Jason, Jamie and Michael continue to surprise and entertain me with their intelligence, drive, compassion and humour. They are such inspirational men and have beautiful partners sharing their lives. I am blessed that Sonic and Skadi chose me to be their gruncle (great uncle), they enrich our lives with endless love and laughter. I also have 3 step kids Nicholas, Yasmina and Dominic who I have had the privilege of watching grow as they discover their roles in this world.

Then there are the other family members who traditionally would not be included, but for me they have been so important in making me the person I am today that I couldn't not include them in my family unit. This includes my ex-wife Julie and her husband Alan who are great friends and continue to support me in my endeavours. Then there is my ex-brother-in-law Pete who remains a firm part of the family. For me the term ex refers to them being exceptional people and not that I have moved past them. Of course I couldn't leave out my dear friend Amalia, who continues to be that person who mocks me as being the real-world Kramer from Seinfeld and laughs at me while still being an avid supporter of my never-ending projects.

Any book is the result of a group of super talented people coming together to support the author's vision. This includes the editors, Penny Carrol, my *Sort your Sh!t Out* editor Lucie Bland and Teagan Kum Sing who worked tirelessly to make sure my words made sense, my PR guru Scott Eathorne from Quikmark Media who pushes me to get my books out into the public arena. Michael McDermaid and Ben Aitchison from Paradigm Print Media also should be recognised for patiently working with me to get my books looking and feeling the way I could have only dreamed of.

"What separates privilege from entitlement is gratitude."
– Brene Brown

About the Author

Gary is someone who stays busy exploring life. When something grabs his attention he can't help but go down the rabbit hole to understand and experience it, which is evidenced by the more than 40 jobs he has done. He currently lives on a farm on the Gold Coast in Queensland with his wife Azra and their two dogs Louis and Daisy.

Born in Brisbane Australia he spent 7 years growing up in Papua New Guinea with his adventurous parents, who instilled their 'give it a go' attitude into their children. His family includes his wife, father, a sister, and while he has no kids of his own, he is blessed with 3 nephews and 2 step kids who he gets to share his adventures, experiences and guidance with. He has experienced altitude sickness trekking through the Himalayas, abseiled down a live volcano, swum with sharks, surfed with dolphins, flies planes, climbed mountains and kayaked through rapids as he explores life.

While his first book Sort Your Sh!t Out was very well received across media resulting in great book sales, Gary is most proud of how he has been able to help so many people reinvent themselves. It is those stories that motivated him to release Mastering the Art of Reinvention. His approach to exploring life has seen him featured on national television for his first book, selling a property as James Bond and launching several start-ups. He has played significant transformational roles across multiple industries including health, technology, finance, consulting, education, and aviation. His life has been one of reinvention both professionally and personally through his successes and failures.

At a professional level, his many different jobs have given him invaluable insights into diverse industries and business models which has allowed him to hone his ability to help others reinvent themselves and get shit done. He is a transformational change specialist who has helped many people and organisations reinvent themselves using his practical expertise and engaging approach. His background has seen him working as a topless waiter, lecturer and CEO advisor. Starting his fulltime working life as a science maths high school teacher, he has had over 44 different jobs throughout his life and earned two master's degrees in business and finance, along with his teaching qualifications.

Gary has been involved in fitness for all of his life and his relaxation passion involves anything to do with water, his adventurous upbringing has instilled in him a love of adventure, travel and discovery as he searches for that perfect surf break.

The Gig Game

RULES OF THE GIG GAME.

1. You must have been paid for the gig.

2. You can't count jobs with the same job title more than once.

3. It doesn't matter if you only lasted at it for one shift or a day, you can still count it. E.g my single Kentucky Fried Chicken kitchen hand shift made the count.

4. As you go through your list, think about what you learned from the gig and how it helped you reinvent yourself to be the person you are.

Milkman	Model	Builder
Presenter	Aerobics instructor	Student
Facilitator	Change Manager	Personal trainer
Bank teller	Advertising consultant	Bouncer
Author	Publisher	Labourer
Kitchen hand	Camp coordinator	Swimming instructor
Actor	Topless waiter	Retail Shop owner
Entrepreneur	Fashion Manufacturer	Consultant
Barista	Compliance Manager	Developer
Shop assistant	Advertising executive	Registered Training
Waiter	Science Maths Teacher	Organisation Manager
University lecturer	Barman	Business owner
Project manager	Writer	Trainer
Strategy consultant	Video producer	Program Director
Food manufacturer	University Lecturer	Camp leader
	Glassie	